Fun! Oh My!

...in from the prairies, Hawaiian...ncers from the islands and ...e chewing gum venders will be ...dence. Balloons and whistles ... procured to amuse the chil...nd also the grownups. ...some things will be absolutely ...get "sold" for your nickel. Nay, ...s at least. In short, the carni...st Friday is going to be the ... greatest affair you will ever ... see or even dream about!

Side Shows

Side Shows are really unique; ...hrongs to them entrance will ...eek. ...e are mummies and snakes, ...none of them fakes; ...ey charge only five cents a ...eek.

Fish Pond

...requires patience and pluck, ...re every fisher has luck. ...u fall in the pool ...l not find it too cool, ...re's no mud in which to get ...tuck.

Chamber of Horrors

Of horrors you'll find here a host. No use of your courage to boast! For when you are through Your face will be blue, As if you had seen your own ghost.

Fortune Tellers

The present, the future, the past May all be discovered at last: The Gypsies of old Our fortunes have told, But Miss Holloway has them out-classed.

Court of Justice

If you get more than one double A, The Justice Court's over this way. A ride in the patrol Will be good for your soul, No matter what people may say.

The Victoriola

If you want to hear Signor Caruso Just step right inside here and do so. The Hawaiian delights in her dances. You just ought to see how she prances.

Hawaiian Show

The Hawaiian delights in her dances. You just ought to see how she prances. The sweet ukulele Makes music so gaily That every one there it entrances.

...ESTRA TO SURPRISE AT ASSEMBLY TODAY

...a delightful surprise at the ...d a well chosen program ...out, the High School Orches...l give its second assembly ...l of the season. The program ...ill be more or less popular ...rhaps two or three classical ...ns which the orchestra have ...up to a high state of perfec-

...selection from Humperdinck's ...and Gretel" ought to be of ...interest to the school as this ...among those which Mr. ...

HIGH SCHOOL CLUB BANQUET TO END REMARKABLE YEAR

Big Gym to Be the Dining Room— Professional Entertainers to Make This a Jolly Affair

By Fred Wilcoxen

Every fellow in school is urged to be present next Monday at the final banquet of the High School club.

Because of the serious trend of the former meetings this culminating banquet will be a jovial affair. Professional entertainers have been secured for and ...

BASKETBALL SEASON OPENS POOR LIGHTWEIGHT PROSPECTS

Big Squad of Midgets and Heavies But Not Enough Lights to Form Two Good Teams

By Ernest Hemingway

A big squad out for midgets, a good squad for heavyweight and a very poor showing for lightweights is the present basketball situation.

Ten teams of six fellows each have shown up for competition in the inter-school league, the schedule of which starts Friday. Huxham, Johnson, Royal, Kernstern, Harter, Brandt, Wilson, Steenburg, Asner and Mc-Guineas have been selected as the captains of the midget teams.

Only twenty fellows have reported for lightweight basketball and Thistlewaite is very disappointed. He says, "Last year there were over fifty fellows out for the minors and the four when we are going to have separate teams, a league team and an independent team, only twenty fellows are out. The members of each team will receive monograms and there is certainly a fine chance for fellows to make the team. Unless more fellows turn out for the intra-school squads from which the independent teams will be picked, the idea will have to be dropped."

The heavyweights have a good lot of material out and prospects of a successful class look bright.

STORY CLUB HEARS PARODY AND SEVERAL STORIES

The Story club held its regular meeting last Tuesday afternoon in the English club room.

The first few minutes were given over to business. Westford Peatee

GIRL'S CLUB STARTS WITH INTERESTING MEETING

Mrs. Dr. Winfield Scott Hall Talks on Journey Through Life and Points Many of the Pitfalls.

By Helen Carr

The Girls' Club, entered on the second year of its existence last Wednesday afternoon, when about two girls gathered in the assembly hall to hear Mrs. Dr. Winfield Scott Hall. The council hopes to secure Miss Sophanisba Breckenridge of the University of Chicago, to address the club at the next meeting.

Mrs. Hall talked to the girls about the journey of life, and its most important stations. She advised them to make sure that they were talking the right train, telling them which one she meant. Her quick wit, and pointed anecdotes drove home the ideas which she wished to emphasize, with unusual force.

At the conclusion of her speech the girls adjourned to the lunchroom to discuss it over the "good eats" that Mrs. Foster had provided.

MEMBER OF PARLIAMENT AT PARENTS-TEACHERS MEET

Francis Nielsen, M. P., the famous author and play writer, will speak at the Oak Park high school assembly at December 6, at 8 o'clock. Mr. Nielsen's subject will be "International-ism and World Peace." He will speak under the auspices of the High School Parents and Teachers' association.

Tickets may be secured at the high school from members of the association. The price is 50 cents and entitles the holder to admission to the lecture and a year's membership in the association.

A Life Lesson

His most vivid illustration was ...en from his own life as a soldier ...the island of Samar, a small island ...the Philippines. A new and ...trained regiment of soldiers ...from the south were relieving ...mesfahr's regiment. Novices in ...art of subduing the head-hunting ...ages and filled with a great idea ...their own ability, the incoming ...ment refused to believe that the ...ages would, if given the opportunity ...rise up and massacre them. The ...pinos were allowed the run of ...camp. The next was just a question ...of time. Three days later they ...beset and massacred by these ...ages and the ...

Hammesfahr...
...ods of driving home their points ...their illustrations are all the ...more forceful they are given from ...sonal experience. "Hammesfahr ...not without sympathy for the fel...and he realized that the fellows ...to learn and they would not be hu...if they did not at times disregard ...vice, however good. His life as ...army man, as secret service agent ...during the last few years inter...in boys and young men, has left ...Hammesfahr with the broadest ...of life.

ERNEST HEMINGWAY'S APPRENTICESHIP

Oak Park, 1916–1917

Hemingway back from the war, 1919

ERNEST HEMINGWAY'S APPRENTICE-SHIP

Oak Park, 1916–1917

Edited by

Matthew J. Bruccoli

 *A Bruccoli Clark Book*

 Microcard Editions

Printed in the United States of America
Published by Microcard Editions,
901 26th Street, N.W., Washington, D.C. 20037
a part of the Industrial Products Division,
The National Cash Register Company

To Joan Scholes

Contents

The Tabula

Foreword

After his early successes in the literary world, Ernest Hemingway made relatively few trips back to Oak Park to visit the community where he grew up. There is a suggestion in all this that he may not have been too happy in the rather restricted environment of a conservative suburban middle class community. Yet the record of his high school experiences tells another story. In talking to his former teachers and classmates and in paging through back issues of the student newspaper and school annual, one can piece together an account of a young boy with an amazing amount of talent and enthusiasm, who seemed to take great joy in the academic, social, literary, and athletic programs of the school.

The variety of Hemingway's extracurricular activities is impressive. He played cello in the school orchestra and received his high school letter as a lineman on the football team. He acted in the senior class play as well as managed the school track team. During his junior and senior years most of his energy seemed to be devoted to literary activities. In the years 1916 and 1917, there was rarely an issue of the school paper that did not contain at least one piece by Hemingway. His contributions to the school literary magazine were impressive. One of his former classmates commented recently that Hemingway "was always in things, and we were laughing at what he wrote or appreciating what he did."

Although the students may have laughed at Hemingway's antics, I understand that there were times when one of my predecessors—Mr. Marion Ross McDaniel—

was not nearly so amused. Mr. John Gehlmann, the advisor to *Trapeze* during Hemingway's senior year, still delights in telling of his difficulties with the superintendent over Hemingway's Ring Lardner imitations. It seems that the language and subject matter of these stories horrified the conservative Mr. McDaniel. One wonders how he would have survived in this day of the student underground newspapers.

But high school for Hemingway was more than just playing football and writing for *Trapeze*. There was also the academic program to contend with. The school had, as it does today, a reputation for being one of the finest public high schools in the country. In Hemingway's time, the graduates of the school were so well prepared academically that they often found the first two years of college repetitious and dull. This fact may have played a small role in Hemingway's decision not to follow through with his plans to attend the University of Illinois. Hemingway's academic record in high school reveals that he was a fine student in all areas. Mr. Frank Platt, Hemingway's former English teacher, can still produce his grade book to prove Hemingway's proficiency in freshman composition.

Of course, we at Oak Park and River Forest High School are very proud to have Ernest Hemingway head our list of distinguished graduates. His influence on our school can be seen today in the importance still placed upon the writing program. *Trapeze* is published on a weekly basis and is one of the finest high school newspapers in the country, and the school literary magazine recently celebrated its 75th year of uninterrupted publication.

In the spring of 1967, the students and faculty of the school demonstrated their pride in Hemingway and his achievement by organizing a series of lectures and symposiums commemorating the 50th anniversary of his graduation from the school. Perhaps the most lively and interesting event in this series was a panel discussion entitled, "Hemingway as We Knew Him: Reminiscences of Hemingway by Teachers, Classmates, and Friends." As part of the commemoration, the school literary magazine republished several short stories which Hemingway wrote during his student days.

In 1969, the Board of Education felt that it was necessary to preserve for posterity the collection of Hemingway materials contained in the school archives. Mr. Daniel Reichard of the school's English Department was appointed to compile and edit for microfilm all the material written by and about Hemingway in the school's publications. The microfilm, entitled *Ernest Hemingway in High School: Writings About and By Ernest Hemingway as They Appeared in the Publications of Oak Park and River Forest High School, 1916-1919*, is a significant and enlightening record of Hemingway's high school life.*

In looking over this material recently I couldn't help but be impressed by the foresight of the editors of the 1917 *Tabula*. They certainly showed unusual perception when they wrote as a tag for Hemingway's picture— "None are to be found more clever than Ernie."

Russell J. Fuog
Superintendent
Oak Park and River Forest High School
Oak Park, Illinois

*This microfilm is available from Oak Park and River Forest High School, 201 North Scoville Avenue, Oak Park, Illinois 60302.

Introduction

Everything Ernest Hemingway wrote is important because he wrote it.[1] That Hemingway opposed republication of his apprentice work matters little now, for it cannot possibly alter his stature. Everything he wrote will be collected sooner or later, and it will give pleasure to general readers and help students to understand his career. If sooner or later—then the sooner, the better.

Hemingway began writing for *The Trapeze* at the start of the second semester of his junior year and contributed 39 pieces by graduation. Under the revolving editor plan in effect, he served as chief editor for some issues. Hemingway was concerned that his early work would somehow be used against him by hostile critics. But his high-school writings are juvenilia and cannot injure his reputation. It would be too much to claim that *The Trapeze* material shows special promise, although the Ring Lardner imitations show Hemingway groping for a style and a satiric stance—and looking in the right place. Indeed, *The Trapeze* writings indicate that at seventeen and eighteen he had no distinction as a journalist: the editorial, "Support the Swimming Team," is pretty awful. Hemingway was a born genius, but as a high-school reporter he had not yet learned what to do with his genius. The real importance of *The Trapeze* material is biographical. Instead of the unhappy loner—the gifted and sensitive adolescent in a square environment—that has been reconstructed, *The Trapeze* shows an active joiner, a big man in the school. Even allowing for the fact that editors of high-school papers always write about each other, the 59 mentions of Hemingway—in addition to work by him—in *The Trapeze* are noteworthy. He attracted publicity, and perhaps the emergence of the "Papa" image can be discerned this early.

The Trapeze material occasionally provides a glimpse of the young man who was uncomfortable with respectability. Although they seem very tame now, his references to drinking—"Hemingway and a full Stein"— were probably upsetting to dry Oak Park. And the Hanna Club articles seem to reveal that Hemingway was beginning to burlesque the Oak Park values while still adopting them: "In fact, it was so great a speech that there was no discussion afterwards"; "Mr. Hammesfahr closed his speech with this illustration, and left the fellows to draw their own conclusions about the value of not smoking, not drinking, and living a clean life. They did."

Hemingway told Charles Fenton—"Christ: The *Tabula*. You know the worst thing you can do to a writer is to dig out his worthless and childish stuff which he deliberately never allows to be collected or republished. It is like publishing the contents of his wastebasket."[2] Some wastebasket. *The Tabula* short stories do show promise and anticipate the material—though not the style—of the later Hemingway. Although these stories are imitative of Jack London and Lardner, they reveal that the young Hemingway had an awareness of the technique of fiction—in particular, of the development of character through speech. The best of the three, "Sepi Jingan," employs a double point-of-view—with a civilized narrator reporting the speech of a semi-civilized protagonist. It is not difficult to see Billy Tabeshaw as a Hemingway code figure.

xiv

The "Class Prophecy" shows Hemingway's enjoyment of rough ad hominem humor, as well as his delight at sneaking scatalogical references into his writing. The account of Printup's "fiery end" is a reference to the flatulent hero of the song "One-Ball Reilly."[3] The *Tabula* poetry—imitative of James Whitcomb Riley and Carl Sandburg—is unremarkable. The most noteworthy thing about it is that it shows Hemingway engaged in a literary activity that probably was not considered part of normal masculine activity by his classmates.

These texts have been printed exactly as they appeared in *The Trapeze* and *The Tabula*. No corrections have been made.[4]

My chief debt is to C. E. Frazer Clark, Jr. for the freedom of his Hemingway collection. The following scholars, librarians, and collectors helped me to locate material: Daniel Reichard, John Via, Audre Hanneman, Donald Gallup, and Waring Jones. Special thanks are due to Jennifer E. Atkinson and I. S. Skelton.

[1]See my Preface to *Ernest Hemingway, Cub Reporter* (Pittsburgh: University of Pittsburgh Press, 1970).

[2]"Ernest Hemingway's Literary Apprenticeship, 1916–1923"—Yale University Dissertation, 1953.

[3]D. E. Wylder, "Hemingway's Satiric Vision—The High School Years," *Rendezvous*, V (Winter 1970), 29–35. See also Daniel P. Reichard, "None are to be found more clever than Ernie," *English Journal*, LVIII (May 1969), 668–672.

[4]Carlos Baker's *Ernest Hemingway A Life Story* (New York: Scribners, 1969) describes on p. 23 a *Trapeze* article about an attempted suicide written by Hemingway in spring 1916. It is not listed by Audre Hanneman (*Ernest Hemingway A Comprehensive Bibliography* [Princeton: Princeton University Press, 1967]); and I have not found it.

ERNEST HEMINGWAY

Class Prophet; Orchestra (1) (2) (3);
Trapeze Staff (3), Editor (4); Class
Play; Burke Club (3) (4); Athletic As-
sociation (1) (2) (4); Boys' High School
Club (3) (4); Hanna Club (1) (3) (4);
Boys' Rifle Club (1) (2) (3); Major
Football (4); Minor Football (2) (3);
Track Manager (4); Swimming (4).

**"None are to be found more clever than
Ernie."**

ILLINOIS

"What sort of shit were you writing when you were 14–15–16 or 17? All I know is that I wrote shit."

Ernest Hemingway to Charles Fenton

The Trapeze

CONCERT A SUCCESS

**Both Musically and Financially the
Symphony Concert on Monday
Evening Won Out**

INTEREST IN VENTURE GROWS

Ernest Hemingway

The Chicago Symphony Orchestra concert was a financial as well as an artistic success. There was a small profit, which will help to make up the deficit from the first concert.

The program opened with a concerto, G Major, by Bach. This was played by the string orchestra and was beautifully given. In the Adagio the violin obligato by the Concert Meister, Henry Wiesbach, was especially well received. Mr. Wiesbach was given excellent support by the entire orchestra. The Allegro of the same concerto showed some excellent staccato work by the violin section.

The second number was the ever-popular Brahmn Symphony No. 2, D Major. The first number of this symphony was played in a great part by the wood winds and French horns. It was followed by the Adagio Non Troppo, with its graceful, rhythmic swing, the allegretto grazio with its pastoral movement and the symphony aided with the allegretto con spirito, which is very syncopated and spirited. The last number was very brilliantly played and was excellently interpreted.

The Siegfried Idyl, Wagner, was not the popular conception of Wagnerian music, it having an

3

easy, smooth flowing motif. It was perhaps the best selection of the whole program.

The concert closed with the Finale from "Die Gotterdammerung," by Wagner. This inspiring piece contains as the ever-recurring theme "Cry of the Valkeries,' 'and it was given as only an orchestra under the direction of Mr. Stock can give it. The selection was masterfully played and closed the finest concert ever given in Oak Park.

The performance was well attended by parents and teachers, but we think that a larger representation of students should have been present. If the next concert is a financial success, Mr. Erickson plans to bring the orchestra out here for an afternoon performance at popular prices.

To all the pupils who can do so, attend the next concert and show that the Oak Park High School students appreciate good music.

———————

HANNA CLUB
TOMORROW NIGHT

———

**Mr. David Goodwillie to Talk—Eats
to Be a Surprise—Jokes and
Good Fellowship Promised**

———

By Ernest Hemingway

One of the disappointments, which were mingled with the blessings of our flood, was the fact that the Hanna club did not meet Friday night, as planned. The postponement, however, only heightened the pleasures of anticipation, for Mr. David Goodwillie's speech on the "Employer and the Employee," which will be given this Friday night. Dinner will be served at 6 p. m. at the lunch room.

No one should stay away because they say they have had dinner at the lunch room at noon; because Friday night there is going to be something different. It would be gladly announced, but Mrs. Foster compels us to keep it secret.

Jokes will be told by the members during the supper, and every member will be expected to come prepared. There is a new Ladies' Home Journal and the Daily News is only one cent, so get busy, fellows. If none of these sources are available, ask Mr. Platt about that Ford story.

President Elton especially wishes Freshmen to come to the meetings. This is the best chance for the Freshmen to meet the upper classmen, and to become acquainted with the best fellows. Also we promise to print in **large, bold face type** the name of the Freshman telling the best joke.

The meeting will be over by 7:30 o'clock, in time for the basket ball game, so there is another excuse gone. Tickets must be purchased by noon Friday, so that Mrs. Foster will know how many to prepare for.

There will be a great speech, a superb dinner, and some rare jokes. So dig down in your watch pocket among the locker keys and Lincoln pennies, and painlessly extract that two bits piece you have been wondering what to do with, and purchase one of those little red pasteboards that will open the gates to an hour and a half of the happiest time you ever spent.

———————

HANNA CLUB MEMBERS HEAR PRACTICAL TALK

———

**Largest Attendance For Years Past
Inaugurate Life Problems Discussions—Debate To-
morrow Night**

———

By Ernest Hemingway

Mr. David E. Goodwillie gave an excellent presentation of the employer's side of the labor problem at the Hanna club, last Friday. He spoke against child labor and he very strongly urged against labor unions. He also spoke against Ford's idea of giving $5 a day to those who do not earn it. He presented in a very concise and foreceful way the business man's standpoint on the problems, and the boys were very interested in his remarks.

Before Mr. Goodwillie's address President Elton gave a short talk on the aims of the club and the place that he hoped it would fill in the school life. On account of the basketball game there was no general discussion after the speeches, but in the future this will be a feature of the program.

A large crowd of fellows attended the dinner and they certainly received their twenty-five cents' worth. After the dinner the crowd all went down to the second floor study hall, where the meeting proper was held. A number of good jokes were told, but the Freshmen, strange to say, did not favor us with any, so that we are unable to print any Freshman's name. After the jokes came the speeches, which have been described.

The attendance was good, the upper classes and Freshmen being well represented. The Sophomore class, however, had very few members present. President Elton announced that the lunch room would serve any menu that the fellows wanted, so any members having suggestions please give them to Mrs. Foster.

At the next meeting the question will be "Which is the better, a practical or theoretical education?" Clyde Reading will give a talk for the practical side and Stewart Hawes for the theoretical. This is sure to be an interesting meeting, and there should be a large attendance. A better representation from the "Boom Bine—Boom Bate" class is desired. Tickets may be purchased until Friday noon, and the price is twenty-five cents.

---

10 February 1916, 1

PRACTICAL EDUCATION
VS. THEORETICAL

———

**Hanna Club, With Largest Attend-
ance in Its History, Enthuse
Over This Question**

———

By Ernest Hemingway

The Hanna club held the liveliest meeting of its
career, Friday night. It was snappy and full of hot
discussions from start to finish, and over half of
the fellows took part.

After the usual good supper, a few jokes were
told, Trafton starring with his story of the "nostril" of the gun. The discussion then began. The
question before the club was: "Which is the
better, a practical or theoretical education in
college?"

Stewart Hawes upheld the theoretical side in a
masterful manner. He spoke against specialization
and said that a fellow should try and obtain a general education so that he would be thus fitted to
take up some special branch of work. He also
spoke of the broadening influence of a classical
education and the essential culture that it imparts
to every man.

Clyde Reading spoke as strongly for the practical side and said that a fellow should specialize
so that he would be able to do one thing well and
not be a "jack of all trades" and master of none.

After the two leaders made their speeches the
hot arguments started. At times four and five fellows would be on their feet at a time and the trend
of argument seemed to be in favor of the practical
side. The theoretical side, however, was ably sup-

9

THE TRAPEZE

VOL. V. NO. 7   OAK PARK, ILL., THURSDAY, FEBRUARY 10, 1916   PRICE 2 CENTS

MIDGETS WIN FIVE STRAIGHT

Trim Deerfield and Lewis by Good Scores—Oak Park Lands in Second Division

BASKETBALL SCHEDULE OUT

Heavyweight

Team—	W.	L.	Pct.
Oak Park	2	1	.667
Thornton	2	1	.667
Bloom	2	1	.667
Morton	0	3	.000

Lightweight

	W.	L.	Pct.
Oak Park	2	1	.667
Morton	2	1	.667
Deerfield	1	2	.333
Bloom	1	2	.333

Basket Ball Schedule

Feb. 11—Bloom at Oak Park. Both teams.

Feb. 19—Oak Park at Thornton. Heavyweight.

Feb. 19—Oak Park at Deerfield. Lightweight.

Feb. 25—Oak Park at Morton. Both teams.

Oak Park's flying lightweights trimmed Lewis 26 to 5 last Tuesday, making it five straight. Holden, a former Oak Park star, scored Lewis' first point with a free throw. Stanley came back for Oak Park with a basket, and Uteritz and Fox made two more. Then Lewis ceased to threat-

A REHEARSAL

WHEN A CLASS PLAY ISN'T A CLASS PLAY

WASHINGTON'S BIRTH-DAY INFORMAL DANCE

General Good Time For All Students Planned by Parents-Teachers' Social Committee

By Susan Lowrey

Here's good news, everybody! The Social committee of the Parents and Teachers' association has planned a big party, for everybody in school, which will take place in the boys' gym, Monday, February 21, after school. It will be a school affair, which means that the Freshmen and Sophs, as well as Juniors and Seniors, will need only to don their tennis shoes, bring a lot of "pep" and come for a good time.

The main entertainment will be

PRACTICAL EDUCATION VS. THEORETICAL

Hanna Club, With Largest Attendance in Its History, Enthuse Over This Question

By Ernest Hemingway

The Hanna club held the liveliest meeting of its career, Friday night. It was snappy and full of hot discussions from start to finish, and over half of the fellows took part.

After the usual good supper, a few jokes were told, Trafton starring with his story of the "nostril" of the gun. The discussion then began. The question before the club was: "Which is the better, a practical or theoretical education, i. college?"

Stewart Hawes upheld the theoret-

GOOD MUSIC AND CUP AWARD

Interesting Assembly With A Popular Musical Program and Scholarship Mixed

FRANCIS LANGWORTHY WINNER

By Frances Coates

The assembly program of last Friday morning proved the most interesting and enjoyable one this year. Mr. Erickson's musical numbers met with immediate success and each number was applauded with appreciative enthusiasm. "The Only Girl" selection, while it was played with spirit, showed evidence of the careful workmanship that marks all of Mr. Erickson's productions. "Shadowland," the catchy fox trot, with its clever "raggy" effects made it agony to be compelled to sit quietly in our seats. The "Aloha Oe Waltz," was rendered all the more beautiful by Nelson Brabrook's solo. The last number, "Semper Fidelis" proved exceedingly popular, calling fourth two encores. The cornet obligatos were played by Moffat Elton, Nelson Brabrook, William Burbank, Chester Radke, and Raymond Thompson.

Honor Seniors Called to Stage

Principal McDaniel then read the names of the Seniors who have attained the grade of 90 in all their subjects for the first semester, during the three and one-half years of their high school course, and

the half ended 12-3.

Lewis braced and held Oak Park scoreless for five minutes. Then Radcliffe took the ball down the floor and made a basket. Stanley threw the ball in on the next play. Fox scored and then Lewis made another. In a mix-up that occurred, Fox was thrown to the floor and had to be carried out of the game. Cole was injected into the fray and the scoring went on.

The line-up:

Oak Park (26)

	B.	T.	F.
Uteritz, lf	5	0	1
Stanley, lf	4	0	1
Fox, c	3	0	0
Bell, rg	1	0	0
Radcliffe, lg	1	0	0
Cole, c	0	0	0

Lewis (5)

	B.	T.	F.
Holden	1	0	1
McEldowney	1	0	0
Jellenech	1	0	0
McCracken	0	0	0
Ward	0	0	0

Showing championship form, the rejuvenated lightweights beat Deerfield 17 to 8. The battered and crippled heavies lost their game, and as a result went into a triple tie for first place in the second division.

The lightweights had an easy time of it, as Deerfield was unable to break up their plays. Oak Park's passing was remarkably accurate and all the team was able to shoot well. Most of Oak Park's score was made in the first half; the team being too willing to take chances with long shots in the second period.

The heavies were fighting to land in the first division, but superior team work on the part of Deerfield, and the poor shooting of Oak Park, coupled with the absence of Steele, spelled defeat. Oak Park was 3 points behind at half time, and fought desperately in the second half to even the count. A flock of Deerfield bas-

(Continued on page 3)

dancing, not a formal parade with programs filled out a week ahead, but "robber's dances," and general mix-ups, where one may see a blushing Freshie whirling around with some tall, no-longer-dignified Senior. Some music will be voluntary, so, please, all you piano-players don't wait for an invitation! We know Kohler will be there and we all know what good music that means.

At Austin High, dances like this are every-week affairs and tickets are issued for the purpose. Each student receives a ticket and goes to dance, not to sit around and watch—a gallery is provided for those who wish to do that. For the rule is: "He or she who refuses to dance even one dance must forfeit his ticket for the next week." So if there aren't enough fellows to "go around," Sarah Maud dances with Cornelia.

At U. High, also, the gym is open every Friday afternoon for a social dance. How would you like Oak Park added to the list? The honorable committee says our dances may be frequent if a big crowd comes out, joins in with spirit and has such a good time that they want more. This is an experimental party, so every-body out! No, you won't be out even a penny—it's free. Also, there is no school the next day, Washington's birthday, so there will be no lessons to get. Now there aren't any excuses, so come on out, everybody, and show 'em what a lot of fun you can have!

PERSONAL

Gladys Ball, '15, has been made a member of the Deltho club of the University of Chicago.

Howard Hales, ex-'16, saved the lives of four children at the Charlton Nursery fire of last Thursday night.

James Adams is very ill with blood poisoning. Harry Redfearn is substituting for him in the class play, in case he is not able to take his part.

Esther McLean, '14, has been chosen as a member of the Quadrangle club at the University of Chicago.

ical side in a masterful manner. He spoke against specialization and said that a fellow should try and obtain a general education so that he would be thus fitted to take up some special branch of work. He also spoke of the broadening influence of a classical education and the essential culture that it imparts to every man.

Clyde Reading spoke as strongly for the practical side and said that he would be able to do one thing well and not be a "jack of all trades" and master of none.

After the two leaders made their speeches the hot arguments started. At times four and five fellows would be on their feet at a time and the trend of argument seemed to be in favor of the practical side. The theoretical side, however, was ably supported by Worthington, Priebe and Shorney, Chappell, Darnall, Henderson, Rogers, Trafton and Pringle spoke for the practical or specializing side. Harold Sampson and Henry Pringle also became embroiled in an argument over the manual department of the high school. During the discussion many new phases and sidelights on the question were brought out by the many speakers, and the fellows were sorry to see the hands of the clock reach 7:30, the time limit for the meeting. Tickets for the next meeting are 25 cents and should be purchased by Thursday night. The subject will be announced later.

Richard Steele, '16, was taken to the hospital last Monday with a serious illness, which will prevent his taking part in the Senior class play. He has had hard luck all year, having broken his leg during the early part of the football season, which kept him out the rest of the fall. He was captain of the basketball team, but could play in but few games before this illness came on, which will keep him out of all athletics the rest of the year.

called them to the platform, amidst the cheers of the whole student body. The following filed to their appointed seats:

Frances Langworthy, Helen Golder, Esther Hebert, Jean Davies, Eleanor Atkins, Margaret Scarritt, Kathryn Tenney, Clara Hoover, Charlotte Dakin, Stewart Hawes, Sibyl de Joannis, Josephine Taylor, Joseph Townsend, Franklin Pearce, Selma Brambach, Jean Plummer and Evelyn Rogovsky.

Mary Carney and Jean Pickett have the average of 90, but they have not been in this school the required three and a half years.

Leroy Grosser Makes Speech

Principal McDaniel then introduced Leroy Grosser, who represented the class of 1915 in the presentation of the scholarship cup. In a very able speech it was awarded to Frances Langworthy, who stands at the head of her class with the splendid average of 95 per cent. He said in part:

"It seems like returning home, after an extended absence, to be here among you this morning. One never appreciates what he has until it is taken from him. When I left this school last June, diploma in hand, I little realized that I would ever miss the school or its surroundings. But I have missed it mightily during the past few months.

"I am more than glad to be here, as the representative of the class of 1915, in presenting to its winner the 1915 scholarship cup.

"This cup was presented to the school by last year's senior class to perpetuate its memory and to promote a high standard of scholarship. It affords me great pleasure to present this token to Miss Frances Langworthy, the senior, who has obtained the highest average during the past three and a half years.

"Miss Langworthy, yours is the honor of being the first to have your name inscribed upon this trophy.

"Accept it with the congratulations of the school and the class of 1915."

ported by Worthington, Priebe and Shorney. Chappell, Darnall, Henderson, Rogers, Trafton and Pringle spoke for the practical or specializing side. Harold Sampson and Henry Pringle also became embroiled in an argument over the manual department of the high school. During the discussion many new phases and sidelights on the question were brought out by the many speakers, and the fellows were sorry to see the hands of the clock reach 7:30, the time limit for the meeting. Tickets for the next meeting are 25 cents and should be purchased by Thursday night. The subject will be announced later.

———————

MR QUAYLE ROUSES HANNA CLUB

Discussed "Business Careers of High School Boys—Attendance Thermometer Going Up

---

By Ernest Hemingway

The Hanna club attendance thermometer is still rising: at first it stood at 95 degrees, then at 100 degrees, and finally at 105 degrees. The heat of the discussion also is keeping pace with the rise in attendance.

Mr. Quayle spoke at the last meeting of the club on the "Business Careers of the High School Boys." Mr. Quayle is superintendent of motive power of the Northwestern railroad, and the keynote of his speech was that every fellow should have will to labor and determination to win.

His talk was short and concise and he made many pithy statements, some of which are as follows:

"Purpose is better than talent."

"If your work is drudgery, quit the job."

"Each day is a stone in the building of character."

"Genius and success are 98 per cent perspiration and 2 per cent inspiration."

Mr. Quayle told of his own life and career, and of his struggle to get an education. He cautioned the fellows against being satisfied with their work because, as he said, "As soon as a fellow begins to be satisfied with his work he is on the down grade." He gave many illustrations of Edison's unfailing industry and his application to his work.

13

ATALANTA TO GIVE COLONIAL PARTY

Martha Washington Ball on Saturday—Rouge, Powder and Beauty Spots to Be in Evidence

By Florence Winder

Here, girls, is something that will interest you intensely, namely, the Martha Washington ball, to be given by the Atalanta Association, Saturday, February 19. As usual, it is to be held in the girls' gymnasium and George and Martha Washington will lead the grand march at half-past two.

It is to be a simple costume party, and not a masquerade. "A white dress touched up with plain or colored cheese-cloth along with a few beauty spots and a can of powder will make a very pleasing costume," explained Miss Hull to a few who inquired how to dress. She also stated that there will be good, lively music rendered by several violins, piano and drum. Nothing has been said about the "eats," but those who attended the Christmas party know that that part of the program will not be a disappointment.

The general idea of this party is so that the girls will become better acquainted with one another, so if you feel "blue" come out and have a royal good time. The Virginia reel will be danced in the honor and memory of our colonial forefather, then the rest of the afternoon will be devoted to the modern dances. From those who joined the association at the first of the school year a simple fee of ten cents will be collected at the door, but on non-members a tax of fifteen cents will be levied.

METHUSELAH'S RIVAL FOUND AT MATH CLUB

Dale Bumstead Uncovers Him by

Slang

O, sweet little girls of high school.
How shocked I am to hear
The horrid slang of high school girls
That each day greets my ear—

A kid you like is called a "peach,"
The other guy's a "mutt,"
A wise one is a "hummingbird,"
A stupid boob's a "nut."

"Bean" is what you call a "knob,"
A nifty lid's a "dream,"
For bum recitation you say "flunked,"
A funny stunt's a "scream."

You call a dub a "piece of cheese,"
A grouch you call a "crab,"
For gathering kale you always say
"A bunch of dough I'll grab."

You say that she has "beat it,"
When you mean that she was went,
A kid with frightened lamps you call
"A pie-eyed innocent."

O, girlies, can the rough stuff,
zit's fierce, without a doubt;
Take it from me, it's awful punk;
Say, kiddoes, cut it out!—Ex.

"What's your name?"
"Helen French."
"Well, what is it in English?"

An Ode to Spring

The birds are ETAOIN wq eRqv
Sprig is here,
The birds are sigig,
Air is balby, sky is blue.
Little brooklets now are running

MR QUAYLE ROUSES HANNA CLUB

Discussed "Business Careers of High School Boys—Attendance Thermometer Going Up

By Ernest Hemingway

The Hanna club attendance thermometer is still rising; at first it stood at 95 degrees, then at 100 degrees, and finally at 105 degrees. The heat of the discussion also is keeping pace with the rise in attendance.

Mr. Quayle spoke at the last meeting of the club on the "Business Careers of the High School Boys." Mr. Quayle is superintendent of motive power of the Northwestern railroad, and the keynote of his speech was that every fellow should have will to labor and determination to win.

His talk was short and concise and he made many pithy statements, some of which are as follows:

"Purpose is better than talent."

"If your work is drudgery, quit the job."

"Each day is a stone in the building of character."

"Genius and success are 98 per cent perspiration and 2 per cent inspiration."

Mr. Quayle told of his own life and career, and of his struggle to get an education. He cautioned the fellows against being satisfied with their work because, as he said, "As soon as a fellow begins to be satisfied with his work he is on the down grade." He gave many illustrations of Edison's unfailing industry and his application to his work.

At the close of his speech he gave the fellows a short talk on the electrification of Chicago railways. In this talk were many interesting statistics and facts. He said in part that electrification was not practical at present on account of the great ex-on Simon Newcomb.

Methuselah's only rival was discovered in the presence of sixty Mathematics club members last Wednesday. Dale Bumpstead proved (?) Mr. Jones to be now old enough to outlive that ancient character.

Mr. Owen discussed "The Training of Simon Newcomb," as had been announced, and brought forth many interesting features. Mr. Newcomb was born of mathematically inclined parents, so we duller students may blame ourselves for the poor selection of ancestors that we made.

So convincingly were the various other propositions proved that hitherto stationary convictions of the equality of one and one were shattered, and one seemed to equal a minus quantity or two thousand at the will of the demonstrator.

It was quite a jump from such deep problems to the frivolity of Valentine refreshments, but several made the leap successfully. Those pink, heart-shaped cakes, served with pine-apple sundaes, by the refreshment committee will long be remembered.

A clearer idea of what the club is doing, and just how interesting the meetings are may be obtained by attending the next meeting, March 8. Please signify your intent to attend this by "telling your teacher," or one of the club officials, so that preparations may be made accordingly.

Life's Mysteries

Freshmen.
Bonnie's coiffeures.
John's dips.
Lunch room hash.
Frances Langworthy's intelligence.
Third periods.

WANTED—A roll top desk by the Trapeze staff. They will pay a reasonable prize to some patriotic person who has one.

Bob McMasters: "To be perfectly Frank, fellows, it can't be Dunn."

Broke His Vow

"I had the pleasure of meeting your husband last night, and he told me all about Florida. He seemed to be full of reminiscences."

"Oh, my; and George said he'd never touch another drop."

He Must Be a Keeper of a Cemetery

G. Shorney, in making an announcement concerning Hanna club: "Mr. Robert Quayle is to speak, and he is sure to be interesting, as he has three thousand men beneath him."

Larson: "Would counterfeit money satisfy debt?"
Co-Pilot of Air Line: "It would satisfy one party."

Freshman: "I think it ought to be warmer in the mountains than in the valley."
Unsuspecting Senior: "Why?"
Freshman: "Because of the mountain ranges."—Ex.

Editors announce that if the readers get tired reading these columns that they will couch them in more restful language.—Ex.

You can lead a horse to water,
But you cannot make him drink.
You can ride a Latin poney,
But you cannot make him think.

Student—Aw, shut up, your the biggest dunce in the room.
Mr. Larson—Boys, boys, don't forget that I'm here.

Admiral (seeing enemy's ship sunk) —"Who fired that shot?"
Old Salt—"The ship's cook, he got the range and stove her in her side."

Mr. Quayle closed his talk with a poem of Robert Service's that was greatly appreciated by the fellows present.

Owing to the Class Play, there will be no Hanna club meeting this Friday. The next meeting, however, will be one of unusual interest and will bring up a question that all the fellows will be able to discuss.

President Elton especially wishes the fellows to purchase their tickets before Thursday, as it is impossible to have the right number of dinners prepared if a number of people rush in at the last moment.

TEACHERS' MASKED BALL

It is evidently becoming quite the fashion for Oak Park high school to have Washington's birthday dances. The Atalanta will start the ball rolling this Saturday afternoon, then the whole school is to enjoy a general jollity on February 21, and on Feb. 23 the lady teachers of the school are to disport themselves in the girls' gym. They especially wish no visitors to be present, as fancy costumes of different varieties will be worn. All of our fair instructors will come masked, and it is doubted whether one will be able to distinguish Miss Dixon and Mrs. Shirley from one another. This party is to be given by the Misses Ritchie, Lucas and Kraemer, limited to the lady teachers alone, with the exception of Mrs. McDaniels, who is to be the guest of honor.

Old-fashioned dances will be the entertainment of the evening, and a number of delicacies from Mrs. Foster's relam are rumored for the refreshments. Many other things may develop which can be more fully published "the day after."

We all agree that the party promises fair to be a "howling success," and we hope that none of the fair ladies will be so worn out with their frivolity that they will be absent Thursday morning.

—M. H.

At the close of his speech he gave the fellows a short talk on the electrification of Chicago railways. In this talk were many interesting statistics and facts. He said in part that electrification was not practical at present on account of the great expense concurrent.

Mr. Quayle closed his talk with a poem of Robert Service's that was greatly appreciated by the fellows present.

Owing to the Class Play, there will be no Hanna club meeting this Friday. The next meeting, however, will be one of unusual interst and will bring up a question that all the fellows will be able to discuss.

President Elton especially wishes the fellows to purchase their tickets before Thursday, as it is impossible to have the right number of dinners prepared if a number of people rush in at the last moment.

———————

PROBLEMS OF BOYHOOD DISCUSSED AT HANNA CLUB

—

**Rev. Gray and Mr. Towle Fill the Bill
As Leaders in the Discussion—
Judge Baldwin This week**

—

By Ernest Hemingway

Rev. A. B. Gray, pastor of the Central Park church, spoke at the Hanna club, in place of Mr. L. C. Towle. Mr. Gray was introduced by Mr. Towle as one of the "big guns" of Chicago, as a speaker, and he certainly had the range and the angle of fire.

Rev. Gray is a former athlete, and he talked to the fellows from a young man's standpoint. He spoke at the first of the ambitions of boyhood, how we all at an early age want to be a fireman, a groceryman, or a conductor. To illustrate this point he read a poem by Riley, about a little boy that wanted to be a grocery man. He spoke of his own "joys" working his way through college, and then came to his big point, that the soul of no one man touches the soul of any other man. Mr. Gray said that initiative, not genius, is what is important in life, and that persistence is what makes men great. He backed these statements up with many convincing proofs, and his talk was appreciated and enjoyed by every fellow in the room. In fact, it was so great a speech that there was no discussion afterwards. Rev. Gray closed his speech with Kipling's inspiring poem, "If."

The usual good supper and good (?) jokes preceded the speech.

The meeting on this Friday is to be addressed

by Judge Jesse A. Baldwin, one of the finest speakers in Chicago. Every fellow that misses a meeting loses just so much from his life, so let' all get out ———etc. Fill in the blank with the conclusion of one of Brabrook's appeals for attendance. Tickets from Shappell, Wilcoxen, Goodwillie, Elton and others.

———————

BIG HANNA CLUB NEETING
HEARS ROUSING TALK

Record Crowd Present to Hear Great
Speech—Season to Be Closed
Friday with Big Banquet

Ernest Hemingway

Exhorting the members to a clean life by example after example, Mr. Hammesfahr aroused the record crowd of 184 at the Hanna club, last Friday night. On account of the large number present the meeting was held in the big Sophomore study hall. Every seat in the room was filled and, after the usual and unusual jokes, President Elton introduced Mr. Hammesfahr. Nick hrabrook led seven 'rahs for "Ham," and then the greatest talk ever given at a Hanna club meeting began.

Mr. Hammesfahr is one of the men high up in the secret service. He is a big, genial man and he interspersed his talk with many jokes. He told how he was at Manila and was called into a conference of all the secret service men there. This was at the time of the Boxer uprising in China, and the United States, Japan, England, Germany, France and Russia were all asked to furnish a body of picked troops to put down this uprising.

The secret service men called into this conference were to pick the troops to represent the United States from the troops quartered in the Philippines. They were to choose men who didn't smoke or drink, and men who did lead clean lives and have some religious conviction. Some of the men at the conference asked Mr. Taft, then the head of the Philippine Islands, who was presiding over the meeting, what he meant by a religious conviction. He replied: "A man with a religious conviction is a man who believes something and then lives the way he believes."

These secret service men were assigned to different regiments and were each instructed to pick a certain number of men who conformed to these requirements to represent the United States in the allied armies. Hammesfahr was assigned to the Fourteenth infantry, stationed at Negarodo Island and, afted living with the men, fighting with them in battle, enduring many hardships and privations with them, he finally picked sixty-nine men.

These men were brought by ship to Hong Kong, where the other American troops and the allied armies were gathered. He spoke of the contrast between the American troops who had been on active service and were in their old, torn uniforms, who had not had a shave for two months, and the trim, finely uniformed British and German troops.

There was great rivalry between the nations as to who would get to Pekin first to relieve the Europeans and Americans besieged there by the Chinese. At the first the Japs led, but the Americans rested on Sunday, and by thus storing up their energy they, by wonderful marching, reached Pekin four days and seven hours ahead of any, and with only four men dropped out on the way, while the English, the next in, had 120 stragglers. The United States troops accomplished their wonderful marching because they marched six days and rested one and because they were not smokers or drinkers.

The American troops were the first to scale the great wall and enter the city, and the armies stayed there five weeks. During this time not a single American was cought looting, while the next army to them in smallness of numbers had to shoot thirty-eight of their men for this or other crimes.

Mr. Hammesfahr closed his speech with this illustration, and left the fellows to draw their own conclusions about the value of not smoking, not drinking, and living a clean life. They did.

The meeting on Friday is to be a big banquet, such as the final meeting of the High School club was, but the price of tickets is to remain the same. Mr. Hanna, whom the club is named after, is to be the speaker, and we should have so many fellows out that we should have to use the assembly room.

————————

JUNIOR DEBATES

Many Juniors wonder what is the use of the Junior debates. We believe that there is no part of the school work more useful and beneficial, and yet more cordially hated than these same debates. A prominent Chicago jurist said recently:

"The training given in the high schools in debating is perhaps the most practical and useful given. It teaches confidence, self-reliance and ease in speaking and informs the pupils on vital topics of the day."

There is also something gratifying in seeing a huge, athletic fellow, who usually emphasizes his remarks by poking his fist under his opponent's nose, be squelched, crushed and verbally sat upon by a little ninety-eight-pound lad who had hitherto been in abject awe of the rough person with the large mouth.—E. M. H.

ATHLETIC ASSOCIATION TO ORGANIZE NEXT WEEK

Plan to Enlarge Membership by Reducing Fee—Officers to Be Elected.

By Ernest Hemingway.

The Athletic Association will reorganize some time next week. At this first meeting of the old members a resolution to reduce the membership fee from fifty cents to twenty-five cents will be introduced by Coach Thistlethwaite. The annual memberships of the association has averaged about 400 and by this reduction of membership fee Thistlethwaite expects to increase the membership to include every fellow in school.

At the initial meeting officers for the ensuing year will be elected and the time set for the second meeting. Meeting number two is very important because at it are held the annual election of basketball and swimming managers. Baseball, track and football managers are not elected until the first meeting after the Christmas vacation.

STOP HELLSTROM.

"Stop Hellstrom and you beat Evanston," is the general verdict of Suburban League coaches. Evanston has a good, hard-playing team but they are not a bunch of world beaters.

Their main reliance on offence is the line bucking and drop kicking of Helstrom. Evanston believes that Hellstrom can hit through any line, but he can be stopped.

The star halfback is not a runner of the wiggling, twisting type, that is so hard to tackle, but is a straight-running, powerful, line bucker.

However, any man of that type, when hit by a hard, clean tackle, goes down for good, and that is what the Oak Park linemen are going to do to Hellstrom.

So far this year Evanston has not run up against a single team that knew how to tackle. They have piled up scores on bunches whose tackles reached out for the man with one hand.

When they hit Oak Park, however, they are going to run up against a real stone wall defensive team and Eldridge, the old Michigan player, predicts that they will be stopped in their tracks.

Eldridge refereed both the U. High Evanston game and the Oak Park-Proviso game and he says: "If Oak Park plays the kind of football against Evanston that they showed against Proviso in the second half, Oak Park should win."

Last year Helstrom was regarded as a phenomenal drop-kicker. So far this year he has not kicked a field goal. He missed seven against U. High and was unable to boot the ball over the bar from the field against Bloom last Saturday.

For the rest of the men on the Evanston team

only one stands out above the average. He is a colored fellow who plays right end. Wilcoxen, one of the best ends in the Suburban league, will play opposite him, however, and Thistlethewaite is not worried over the question of superiority.

If Oak Park plays the type of football that they have been showing in the second halves of their games from the very start of the Evanston contest they will return the winners.

E. H.

AIR LINE

The following poem was submitted by Ernest Hemingway:

"   "
   !   :   ,   .
    ,   ,   ,   .
  ,   ;   !
    ,

          E. H.

————————

As you will probably notice the above poem is blank verse.

————————

17 November 1916, 1 & 3

OAK PARK VICTORS OVER WAITE HIGH

**Come from Behind and Roll Up
Three Touchdowns in Final Quarter—Speed Wins the Game.**

TOLEDO TEAM VERY HEAVY

By Ernest Hemingway.

By a great spurt in the final quarter, Oak Park heavyweights defeated Waite High School of Toledo by a count of 35–19. Waite had a strong hard-fighting team and might have been victorious if they had not tried forward passes in the last part of the final quarter. After three quarters of play, during which the lead constantly changed hands, Oak Park came into the middle of the last period with the short end of a 19–14 score. Waite had the ball on Oak Park's 40-yard line. Trout attempted an end run but fumbled and Gordon scraped up the ball and raced 60 yards for a touchdown. Shepherd kicked goal and Oak Park went into the lead, 21–19. During the remaining seven minutes of play Oak Park acquired two more touchdowns by Kendall's and Bell's anticipation of forward passes.

Featured by Open Play.

The game was hard-fought throughout and was featured by the open fieldrunning of the Oak Park backs and the line plunging of the heavy Toledo back field. Cole, Savage, Timme, Shepherd, Kendall and Wilcoxen stood out as the individual luminators for Oak Park while Twist and Rouch starred for Toledo.

Twist and Rousch are the two most powerful line smashers Oak Park has stacked up against this year and they made many long gains on smashes through the Oak Park forward wall.

Oak Park far outclassed Toledo in the execution of end runs and in handling forward passes and it was this superiority that won them the game.

Play by play account of the game follows:

First Quarter.

Captain Foster of Waite won the toss. He chose to defend the last goal. Golder made a pretty off side kickoff, the ball rolling the required distance. Savage fell on the ball in midfield. On two line bucks Oak Park failed to gain. On a punt formation Cole ran around Clemens to Waite's 30-yard line. Two tries at the line failed. On a punt formation Cole ran around right end to Waite's 31-yard line. Two line plunges failed. Shepherd tried a place kick but the pass fell short and the kick was blocked.

Young fell on the ball on Toledo's 40. On successive line plunges Waite carried the ball to Oak Park's 45. Waite's interference was using its hands and was penalized 15. Foster punted to Phelps, who was thrown on his 20. Cole punted on the first play to Simpson and the Waite quarter returned to Oak Park's 45.

Waite gained 25 in the exchange of punts. Plunges into the line put the ball on Oak Park's 40. Waite was off-side and it cost the East Siders five. A lateral pass was tried. Simpson being thrown back for a loss of 10. Then Foster booted to Cole, who was thrown on his 30. Cassidy was off-side for Waite and the ball was advanced five yards.

Savage tried a run around Clemens, but was stopped in his tracks. Foster and Cassidy were hurt. Cassidy left the game. Baumgartner went in at right tackle.

28

Phelps Injured.

Phelps was knocked groggy by a kick on the head and was replaced by Kendall. Cole kicked to Simpson, who was thrown on his 25-yard line. Line plunges brought Waite a first down. A run by Simpson and another by Rouser made another first down. On an off-tackle play Trout went through the left side of Oak Park's line for seven yards. Time was called for the first period.

Score, Oak Park 0, Waite 0.

Second Quarter.

Trout failed at the line. On the fourth down Simpson was thrown for a loss and the ball went to Oak Park. Cole kicked to Foster, who returned to mid-field. A beautiful forward pass, Foster to Clemens, went through. The Waite end ran to the seven-yard mark. The plunging Trout then took the ball and went through the line for a touchdown. Foster failed at goal. Score, Waite 6, Oak Park 0.

Foster kicked off to Worthington, who passed to Kendall. A forward pass grounded. Oak Park was off-side and was set back five yards. Savage ran around right end to Waite's 40. Kendall made five. Then Waite was penalized 10 for piling up on the man with the ball. Savage next took the ball and ran between Lochart and Young for a touchdown. Shepherd kicked goal. Score, Oark Park 7, Waite 6.

Oak Park in Lead.

Worthington kicked off to Simpson, who came back to mid-field. Oak Park was docked 15 yards for unncessary roughness. A forward pass grounded and Trout failed at the line. Rousch went through the left side for a first down. Simpson lost five yards, Wilcoxen nailing him. Foster tried to chop kick from the 45-yard line. Oak Park blocked the boot and recovered the ball.

Gets On Waite's Ten-Yard Line.

On a triple pass Cole went around left end for eight. Timme hit the center for first down. Then Cole went around Clemens to Waite's 46. Wilcoxen took a forward pass to the 30. Timme received another and ran to Waite's 10. Sheets replaced Simpson. Timme made a yard and Savage three.

Cole threw a forward pass over the goal line that grounded for a touchback. The ball was brought out 20 and given to Waite. End runs by Rousch and Sheets made the first down. Trout made six through center. Foster was thrown for a seven-yard loss on an attempted forward pass. Then Foster punted to Kendall in mid-field. On a forward heave Gordon ran to Waite's 20. Another pass was intercepted by Sheets, who ran it back to his 30.

Rousch was hurt making a yard. On a double pass Sheets tore around end for a first down. Rousch slipped by end to Oak Park's 37-yard line. Cole intercepted a pass by Foster and was downed on his 15. Cole booted out of danger. Oak Park recovered a fumble. Kendall sprinted around left end to Waite's 15-yard mark. Golder was replaced by Hill. Time was called for the half. Score, Oak Park 7, Waite 6.

Third Period.

Foster kicked off to Wilcoxen. He returned to the 31. Savage made five and Timme four. Cole went around Clemens to Toledo's 28. On an attempted double pass on the fourth down Oak Park fumbled and it was Waite's ball.

Rousch made seven. Young failed on a tackle play. A forward pass from Foster put the ball on Oak Park's 20. With a yard to go on the fourth down, Trout went through Dunning to the five. Oak Park was off side and the ball was put on its one line. Sheets went through center for a touchdown. Foster goaled. Score, Waite 13, Oak Park 7.

30

Foster kicked to Wilcoxen, who came back to his 35. Cole kicked to Sheets, who ran to his 30-yard line. Rousch and Trout made first down for Toledo. Sheets fumbled. Danning fell on the ball and then picked it up and ran unmolested over the goal line for a touchdown. Shepherd kicked goal.

Score, Waite 13, Oak Park 14.

On the kickoff Worthington booted over the goal line for a touchback. The ball was brought out 20 yards and given to Waite. By steady line plunging, principally by Rousch, the East Siders carried the ball to their 45. Oak Park stiffened and Foster kicked to Cole, who came back to his 25. Oak Park advanced to its 35, where time was called for the quarter. Total score: Waite 13, Oak Park 14.

Fourth Quarter.

On the fourth down Cole booted to Sheets, who was thrown on his 45. Two dashes by Rousch and a plunge by Trout placed the ball on Oak Park's 40. Trout carried the ball twice in succession and placed it on the visitors' 27.

Two more slams into the line and the ball was on Oak Park's 10. Rousch hurt his ankle. Sheets made a yard. Foster went to Rousch's half, Segrest to fullback. On the next play Trout went through center for a touchdown. Foster punted out and then missed goal. Score, Waite 19, Oak Park 14.

Garry replaced Sullivan for Waite. Foster kicked off to Shepherd, who fumbled on his 45, Waite recovering the ball. Colvin went in at left tackle for Waite.

Fumble Is Costly.

On the fourth down Trout fumbled. Coudon recovered the ball and ran 60 yards for a touchdown. Shepherd goaled. Score, Oak Park 21, Waite 19.

Worthington kicked off to Siegrist, who ran back to Oak Park's 45. On a forward pass Kendall

31

intercepted and raced down the field for a touchdown. Shepherd kicked goal. Score, Oak Park 28, Waite 19.

After Shepherd's kickoff Foster pulled a 35-yard pass to Clemens, who ran to Oak Park's 20.

Another forward pass was fumbled by Lockhart. Bell picked the ball out of the air and dashed 80 yards for a touchdown. Shepherd goaled. Score, Oak Park 35, Waite 19.

Overstreet was replaced by Hemingway. Worthington kicked off. Waite brought the ball back 15 yards. A lateral pass failed. Moore went in for Dunning. Colville replaced Gordon. Foster then kicked to Timme, who was downed on his 30. Oak Park made 3 yards on a line buck. Time was called for the end of the game.

The line-up:

Oak Park—Wilcoxen, l.e.; Worthington, l.t.; Golden-Hill, l.g.; Shepherd, c.; Overstreet-Hemingway, r.g.; Danning-Moore, r.t.; Gordon-Colville, r.e.; Cole, q.b.; Phelps-Kendall, l.h.; Savage-Bell, r.h.; Timme, f.b.

Referee, Haggerty; umpire, King; head linesman, Goodsite; touchdowns, Danning, Savage, Bell, Kendall, Gordon, Trout 3; goals after touchdowns, Shepherd 5, Foster 1; time of periods, 15 minutes.

———————

A "RING LARDNER" ON THE BLOOMINGTON GAME

Right half Smearcase of Bloomington kicked off to Cole who returned the ball to his own one-yard line. Wilcoxen signalled for the hit and run play but Gordon was caught at second by a perfect throw from the catcher. Hemingway went over for the first touchdown by way of the Lake Street "L." Colville missed goal, the ball hitting the bar and causing havoc with the free lunch.

Score, Oak Park 6, Bloomington 0.

Wilkins replaced Cole. Blum kicked off to fullback Roquefort of Bloomington, who was nailed in his tracks. Baldwin of Oak Park wielded the hammer. On the first ball pitched Limburger cracked one to Moore, who stepped on the bag and shot to Wilcoxen at first, doubling the runner.

Savage tried a drop kick from the 90-yard line but it went foul by three inches. Timme then smashed through center for 110 yards for Oak Park's touchdown. Thistlewaite kicked goal.

Score, Oak Park 13, Bloomington 0.

Time was called but refused to answer.

Second Quarter

Lofberg went in at Worthington's tackle. Kendall kicked off to Eycleshymer's front porch. Ball was run back by Quarterback Cambrian to Oak Park's line of demacration. Thistlewaite on incomplete returns claimed three precincts out of 1,396. Hemingway made a tackle. Miss Biggs fainted. Thistlewaite was carried unconscious from the field. Time was called while Fat Tod sent out for a package of **censored** * Maker's name furnished **on request.**

Dunning kicked out of Danger and Lofberg shot a basket from the middle of the field.

Score, Oak Park 15, Bloomington 0.

The captains matched pennies to see who would kick off. Shepherd lost and Bloomington kicked to Phelps, who knocked a clean threebagger, scoring Bell, George and Golder. Hill popped to the pitcher.

Score, Oak Park 18, Bloomington 0.

Wilcoxen went color blind and tackled the water boy. Canode went in at Fullback. The lighting fast Hemingway scored Oak Park's third touchdown, crossing the goal line by way of the Chicago avenue car line, transferring at Harlem and Lake.

Thexton missed goal, the ball striking the bar and falling to the brass rail.

Score, Oak Park 24, Bloomington 0.

Overstreet kicked the ball outside the field and was penalized twenty-seven yards for unnecessary roughness. Wilcoxen again went color blind and tackled a goal post. He was penalized thirty-eight yards for holding.

"Dope" MacNamara replaced the slight Wilkins, who was injured by a kick in the middle of the line of scrimmage.

The game broke up in a riot when the student Cops refused to keep the crowd off the field unless they were given Major Monograms as a farther incentive.

Final score:

Oak Park 24, Bloomington 0.

Late Bulletin

Hemingway is reported as convalescing, but the Doctors Fear his mind is irreparably Lost.

LATER

A large and enthusiastic crowd attended Hemingway's Funeral. A pleasant Time was had By all. _____

34

24 November 1916, 1 & 4

MIDWAYITES DOWNED BY OAK PARK TEAM

**Finishes Suburban Schedule With
Best Score of Season—Team Work
Smooth and Fast.**

COLE AND SAVAGE IN STELLAR ROLES

By Ernest Hemingway.

Scoring nine touchdowns and kicking seven goals, Oak Park smothered U. High by a 61–0 score.

The suburban preps scored in every quarter and the Midway team was powerless to stop the open field running of the Oak Park backs. Savage and Cole made all the touchdowns, Savage getting five and Cole four. These two players made some wonderful sprints of almost the entire length of the field to score the markers. Cole lead with a 95-yard dash through the entire U. High team and a couple of other spurts of almost equal distance. Savage's runs were not quite so long but were equally spectacular. In addition, Savage played a fine defensive game and was the most consistent ground gainer on the team.

Timme played the best game he has show this year and smashed the U. High line to pieces for many long gains. He also contributed to the spectators' enjoyment by staging an eighty-yard run through the center of the U. High line.

Kendall played his usual consistent game and pulled off several long gains. But for hard luck he certainly would have broken into the touchdown column.

35

The Maroon preps were powerless to gain through Oak Park's stone wall forwards. Every player in the line acquitted himself well while Shepherd and Wilcoxen appeared in Stellar roles.

Captain Shepherd played a whiz of a game on defense and added seven points to Oak Park's score by booting goals after touchdowns. The long left end showed up in great style during the first half but was forced to leave the game by injuries just before the end of the second period.

There is not much to tell in regard to the game except that which deals with the individual prowess and machinelike teamwork of Thistlewaite's men.

Oak Park never lost possession of the ball after receiving the kickoff until Savage planted it behind the U. High goal after a steady drive down the field. From then on it was a long succession of touchdowns with Savage and Cole alternating in the scoring. Oak Park did most of their scoring from the middle of the field or beyond. Gordon's work at right end was a feature. The lightweight backfield showed their ability in the last quarter.

The line-up follows:

Oak Park—Wilcoxen-Colville, l.e.; Worthington-Lewis, l.t.; Hill, l.g.; Shepherd, c.; Todd-Overstreet, r.g.; Hemingway-Dunning, r.t.; Gordon, r.e.; Cole-Uteritz, r.h.; Kendall-Phelps, l.h.; Savage-Bell, r.h.; Timme, f.b.

U. High—Rowes, Donahue, l.e.; Blackwood, l.t.; Flack, l.g.; Eastman, c.; Jameison-Sippy, r.g.; Hoyne, r.t.; Van Buskirk, r.e.; Graham, q.b.; MacKevit, l.h.; Harris, r.h.; Mohr, f.b.

Touchdowns—Cole (4), Savage (5); goals after touchdowns, Shepherd (7). Referee, Tapp; umpire, Cook; head linesman, McMurdy; time of periods, 15 minutes.

———

36

ATHLETIC NOTES.

Ernest Hemingway.

The much touted Graham of U. High didn't gain enough ground against Oak Park Saturday to make a bed for Chester Clifford.

A squard of 19 players will make the trip to Bloomington Saturday.

Official pictures of the Major and Minor football teams were taken Wednesday afternoon.

Including last Saturday's game, Oak Park has scored 201 points against its opponents' 66.

Minor basketball practice is already under way and Major practice will start Monday.

The coming number of The Tabula will be an athletic feature edition.

According to figures based on comparative scores, Oak Park could beat Evanston now by a margin of 32 points. Also Englewood by 31 points.

As far as the trap shooting club can find out there is no gun club at Bloomington, so the knights of the shotgun will leave their weapons at home.

According to the dope, Oak Park should win handily over Bloomington but Thistlewaite is taking no chances.

A hockey field is lined off on the new Athetic field for the use of the girls' gymnasium classes.

The finals in the Inter-class Football league were postponed until Monday.

AIR LINE

"Oh, hell! what have we here."

E. H.

(How could you, E. H. Just because this is quoted from Shakespeare do you think it is quite proper for our young minds.)

Found at last, some poetry for the Air Line.

Dedicated to F. W.

Lives of football men remind us,
    We can dive and kick and slug,
And departing leave behind us,
    Hoof prints on another's mug.

E. H.

BASKETBALL SEASON OPENS POOR LIGHTWEIGHT PROSPECTS

———

**Big Squad of Midgets and Heavies
But Not Enough Lights to Form
Two Good Teams**

———

By Ernest Hemingway

A big squad out for midgets, a good squad for heavyweight and a very poor showing for lightweights is the present basketball situation.

Ten teams of six fellows each have shown up for competition in the inter-school league, the schedule of which starts Friday. Huxham, Johnson, Royal, Kernstern, Harter, Brandt, Wilson, Steenburg, Asner and McGuineas have been selected as the captains of the midget teams.

Only twenty fellows have reported for lightweight basketball and Thistlewaite is very disappointed. He says, "Last year there were over fifty fellows out for the minors and the year when we are going to have separate teams, a league team and an independent team, only twenty fellows are out. The members of each team will receive monograms and there is certainly a fine chance for fellows to make the team. Unless more fellows turn out for the intra-school squads from which the independent teams will be picked, the idea will have to be dropped."

The heavyweights have a good lot of material out and prospects of a successful class look bright.

———

OUR "RING LARDNER" JR. BREAKS INTO PRINT WITH ALL-COOK COUNTY ELEVEN

By Ernest Hemingway

ALL-COOK COUNTY TEAM.

Right end .... Cole, Grove
Right tackle .... Hill, Lombard
Right guard .... Goldberger, Oak Park
Center .... Herb Fay, '16, Park
Left guard .... Todheimer, Kenilworth
Left tackle .... Hemingstien, Kenilworth
Left out .... Overstreet, Ontario
Quarter back .... Musselman, Grove
Way back .... Printup, Grove
Half full .... MacNamara, Capt., O. P.
Very fullback .... Hemingway, Kenilw'th

After long and careful deliberation, much study of plane geometry, Robert's Rules of Order, after careful reading of the Christian Herald, Advance and Cosmopolitan, and after conferences with Miss Hull, Miss Dixon, Sue Lowrey and Harry MacNamara, and after attending the Story club and the Burke club, we feel confident that we have done our best in the selection of the above All-Cook County team.

We feel perfectly impartial in this selection because we have never seen any of the players in action when we could help it. In all places we have tried not to have our judgment influenced by the team selected by Mr. MacNamara, of the "Tribune," but in the case of awarding the Full Back job we heartily agree with him.

Cole is the lightest end in the Suburban league.

His recent rise to $17 a ton places him head and shoulders above all the other ends and gives him a great advantage in catching passes. Burch Corl is his nearest rival but we understand corl is lower than before.

Cole has the fire, hard-hitting qualities and consistency that are needed in an all-county end. Hill is placed at right tackle because it would be impossible to gain through him and the opposing back field would become bushed climbing over him.

The three Hibernians—Goldberger, Todhiemer and Hemingstien—are given the two guard jobs and the other tackle position. No team would make any gains off a trio with names like those.

Center position is anonymously awarded to Herbert Fay of 1916, who was the most accurate and consistent passer in the league. Last year against U. High he issued 16 passes and playing La Grange he passed 14 men. All coaches unite in handing him the job.

Overstreet is at left out because we are jealous of him on account of the fact that he beat us in a foot race at Bloomington. Bunny Gilbert, who owes us two bits, is his closest rival.

Quarter back job is yielded to Musselman, who wins the gold enameled can opener. As a quarter back Musselman was the best and most comprehensive air-line pilot ever seen on a local gridiron.

Printup, the modest violet of the Suburban league, is given the position of way back. Shorney, '17, and Reading, '16, were the runners up but Hale was the class of the field.

Because of his masterful selection of an All-County team for The Events, and his public speaking ability, Harry MacNamara is unanimously awarded the position of half full on this honorary

42

eleven. Mac has certainly earned the place and we give him also the honor of the captaincy.

Selecting a full back was the easiest task attempted. His work in English VI., his kicking ability and his stories in The Trapeze make Hemingway the logical choice.

Coach Thistlewaite, in commenting on this star's work at this position, said in part:

"In regard to Hemingway's playing at full back I can honestly say that I have never seen anything like it before in my life! If all backfield men had played like him I cannot begin to prophecy what kind of a team we should have had!"

Hemingway for track manager.—Adv.

ATHLETIC NOTES.

By Ernest Hemingway.

Track practice will begin immediately after Christmas vacation.

Lloyd Boyle and Lloyd Golder are candidates for baseball manager.

It is reported that "Fat" Todd will return to school next year.

Fred Wilcoxen has sent to Ohio for his .12-guage trap gun, as he is dissatisfied with the .20-guage he is now shooting.

Football and soccer pictures may be ordered now, 75 cents apiece.

Oak Park is expected to have the best light-weight basketball team this year it has ever turned out.

A great number of High School fellows are enjoying the skating on the park lagoons.

Basketball shirts were given out last night to the first lightweight team.

Captain White of the swimming team has been unable to practice with the squad, as he is suffering from a severe sore throat.

Savage and Ohlsen nearly severed friendly relations Tuesday during a hot argument about who was the best trap shot.

Mills of the swimming team is showing fine form in the fancy diving event.

George Madill, who was playing on the Fuller Morrison hockey team, is seriously ill with pneumonia.

Edwin Gale may go to White Lake, Mich., on a hunting trip during the Christmas vacation.

Moore and Kraft should make a great showing for Oak Park this year in the middle and long-distance events.

Mathews in the high jump and Pentecost in the broad jump also look good for a lot points.

Oak Park will have a lot of fast men in the dashes this year.

Thistlethwaite expects to develop Wilcoxen into a weight man.

Phelps and Printup were selected by Engel of the Tribune to play on his 1st and 2nd all Cook County lightweight team.

PERSONAL

—

By Ernest Hemingway.

Joseph H. Muir was elected President of the Epworth League of the River Forest M. E. Church.

Miss Ruth Joyce gave a bunco party at which ten couples were entertained at her home last week.

Chester Clifford has returned to school after an absence of two weeks caused by an attack of chicken pox.

The Trapeze extends the sympathy of the School to William Phelps for the loss of his mother and to Warren Davis for the loss of his father.

Philip White, Captain of the swimming team, was given a trial athletic membership by Swimming Coach Hazelhurst of the Hamilton Club.

Elwyn Simmons, '15, is a candidate for the football managership at Illinois U.

Ward Erwin, '18, has returned to Oak Park High School.

William Morganstern, '16, visited school on Friday afternoon.

There will be an Atalanta skating party at Garfield Park, Saturday, January 27.

Winifred Barton, Helen Veatch, Dorothy Hollands, Zelma Owen, and Edith Ebersold put on a skit for the Freshman party.

Helen Nye, 1919, color bearer, slipped as she was alighting from her machine in front of the Oak Park club last Friday night and broke her arm.

Fred Wilcoxen is reported to have won last

week's trap shoot with 48 out of 50 birds smashed. The high cost of shells kept the competing field down to four fellows. Savage, Musselman and Pashley finished behind Wilcoxen in the order named.

Ed Payson, '13, is playing basket ball for Beloit College.

Coach Armstrong has entered serveral men in the Second Regiment Armory meet Friday night.

Joseph Kettlestrings, '20, Dick Hill, '20, and Merrill Smeeth, '20, spoke at the Plymouth League of the First Congregational church Sunday.

Fred Ross and Joel Crissey are giving a 99c dance at the Suburban Club February 7th.

Marshall Wilson spoke Friday night before the Illinois State Y. M. C. A. committee at the Union League club. His subject was "The Boys' Conference".

Sue Lowrey and Franklin Lee attended "The Boomerang" Friday evening.

––––––––––––

GUN CLUB DEFEATS EVANSTONS AND WILMETTE IN TRIANGLE MEET.

———

The Oak Park Gun Club copped the honors in the three cornered meet with Evanston and Wilmette when Wilcoxen and Hemingway took first honors. Wilcoxen dropped 47 out of 50 and Hemingway 46 out of 50 from the 19 yard line. Evanston was second and Wilmette third.

———————

Attributed to Hemingway by Hanneman—C 18.

2 February 1917, 4

'RING LARDNER JUNIOR" WRITES ABOUT SWIMMING MEET. OAK PARK RIVALS RIVERSIDE

Dear Pashley:

Well Pash since you have went and ast me to write a story about the swimming meet I will do it because If I didn't you might fire me off the paper and then when I would want to sling the stuff that Perkins the new air line pilot is named after I would have to go and be a military lecturer or something.

You see Pashley everytime I write anything for your paper a lot of guys want to clean me so this time I will be very careful and only write about myself and about guys what I ain't ascairt of.

Evanston wasn't no meat for us in that swimming meet. But if we would have got 20 more points we would have beat them and If I had have gone 15 feet more I would have won the plunge and If Hughes would have carried 4 more states he would have been elected.

But then as the Bible says there aint no good in crying over split milk or split skirts or something I forget what. There was an Evanston guy to the meet by the name of Kohler and he was some plunger. Why that bird would just flap in the water and float on down to glory and fame at the other end. But that guy will never beat us again because Jack Pentecost and I have fixed up a swell scheme.

There is a black line painted on the bottom of

49

the tank running from one end to the other. Well we will put in a running belt along this line and then Kraft and I will plunge and grab the moving line and get towed along clean to the end of the tank. That is a swell scheme Pash, so keep it dark and don't leave nobody know about it.

But here is another scheme so that we can win swimming meets without Gale being on the team. We will have special events introduced such as
(1) Throwing the Bull (Free Style)
(2) Throwing the Bull (For Time)
(3) Splitting the Infinitive
(4) Rolling the Pills (For Time)
(5) Slinging the Suds (Handicap)
In the first event we could enter R. Harry McNamara, you and me. In the second Le Roy Huxham ought to get first sure. In the third I would bet my last cent that Mickey Kenney would win and in the last two Coxey Muir would start at scratch.

These here extra events would give us a lot of extra points and then we would win the meet sure! But I suppose I had better close now Pash because If I revealed any more of our plans you might leave some of the other schools know and besides I have got to study my Millinery Training for tomorrow because we must save the country no matter at what cost.

Yours Res'y,

Ernest Hemingway.

P. S.—Please leave the printer make some extra copies of the paper because I will want to send them to my friends back in the old town.
Yours, E. H.

P. P. S.—I interviewed a lot of Prominent men on the meet and this is what they said.

50

Coach Reynolds, "___ ___ ___ ! !"
Cap White, "___ ___ ___
___ ___ ___ ! ! ! ! !"
Stew Standish, "___ ___
___ ___ ___ ___ ! ! ! ! !"
Mr. Platt, "On the one hand, yes. On the other hand, No."
R. Harry McNamara, "I concede the election!"
De Veve George, "Carol brothers Carol!"
Marcelline Hemingway, "Yes He's a very distant relative of mine!"
Cap Steever, "It's a man's game!"

E. M. H.

_____

INTERCLASS MEET SATURDAY

Ernest Hemingway.

Oak Park's annual interclass track meet will be held at 10 a. m. Saturday morning in the gym. This meet is open to everyone in school but any man who has won a monogram in a certain event cannot compete in that event.

In this way new stars will have a chance to show up and everybody in an event will have an equal chance.

Coach Armstrong hopes to discover many new track stars in this meet and a large number of entries are expected.

Interclass track meets at Oak Park have never been very successful heretofore because new athletes have not cared to compete against the veterans in the different events. By this new plan which is used in all the big universities a lot of good talent is expected to come out.

ATHLETIC NOTES.

By Ernest Hemingway.

Four former Oak Park stars are showing up well in winter athletics at Illinois U. Bob Tutwiler is out for basketball, Chester Kriedler is doing great work in the broad jump, Reynold Kraft is running the half mile and Waldo Ames recently broke the world's 50-yard indoor hurdle record.

Mr. Baker, head of the Oak Park Boy Scouts, was one of the officials at the big Second Regiment Armory meet Saturday night.

Morris Musselman, leading breast stroke swimmer on the Oak Park squad, may try for a C. A. A. athletic membership.

L. McGrath, Vernon Swanson, Jack Pentecost and Chas. Cusack are the leading candidates for pole vault.

Edwin Gale hopes to make up his condition in German in time to compete in the Interscholastic meet.

A track meet has been scheduled with Nicholas Senn High School for March 3, to be held at Bartlett gymnasium.

John Ritchie is doing cross-country running at Princeton.

Al Eissler, George Yardley, Red Mower and Shorty O'Conner are playing on the Grace church all-star basketball team.

———————————

SUPPORT THE SWIMMING TEAM.

You all know the old "Everybody come out and give the team a little support" stuff. Nearly all our embryo journalists end their impassioned appeals with it. It has become a precedent so we will stick it in now so you will know what kind of an article this is.

But really, you ought to give our splashers the double 0. There is nothing more interesting to watch than a swimming race; if you have never seen one you have missed a lot. At a meet there are always at least five different racing events and very one a thriller! Besides the raccs there is fancy diving. Regular "Daughter of the Gods" stunts. If you have never seen Millsy or Ellis do a "one and a half" you can't realize the thrills you haven't had.

And believe us, the fellows sure will appreciate it if you go out to New Trier with the team at 5:30 o'clock from the Avenue station tonight.

Your rooting may be what will give Stew Standish the final drive to beat out that New Trier guy for first, or make Cap White nose out his man in the relay.

So for John sake show up at 5:30 at Avenue.

See "Ring Lardner, Jr., Discourses on Editorials," 16 February.

ATHLETIC NOTES.

—

By Ernest Hemingway.

Morris Musselman is unable to swim in the breast stroke against New Trier tonight.

Weston Moore is again up in his studies and his return brings joy to the track squad.

Erving Ellis will take Musselman's place in the relay Friday night.

A water basket ball team is about to be organized by Coach Reynolds of the tankers.

Base ball practice will start soon in the gym.

Many Oak Park students have been enjoying the skating at Garfield during the last cold snap.

Some good talent was uncovered in the inter-class track meet Saturday.

RING LARDNER, JR., DISCOURSES ON EDITORIALS

———

Dear Sue—:

Well Sue as you are the Editor this week I thot as how I would write and tell you about how successful I was with my editorials so you would be cheered up and feel how great a responsibility you have in swaying the public opinions.

You know last week I wrote an editorial on Support the Swimming Team.

And in it it told about how swell and exciting a swimming meet was and how thrilling it was and how the team would appreciate peoplc's coming out and everything like that.

It seemed like a hot editorial and I thot gee! there will be a howling mob of rooters at the station for the team and when I came there the platform will be rocked by cheer after cheer.

So I got a very jazzy speech all ready to say and it was to start like this. Before I begin, comma, I would like to explain, comma, that this speech is an oration of the fervid, emotional type, comma, so much in vogue, comma, at the time of Henry Ward Wagenknecht, period.

And I expected at least 500 people and had my speech all ready and do you know how many guys there was there?

There was one guy and it was Savage and I knew that Savage never read no editorials.

Well Sue this here is a time of great public danger and everybody had ought to do his part and so I must do my part to preserve this here nation.

I will write editorials!

First I will write one telling all the German

soldiers to come over here and we will give them free beer, then the Germans will all right away climb up on the top of the alps so as to get as far from here as possible and then I will read them another editorial telling them to hold on tight and they will all let go and drop into the Rhine and be drowned and their dead bodies will be washed down into the Helespont.

And in this way our country would be saved and it would show the power of the press. Is that not a good Idea do you not think?

Well Sue I had better close now on account that I want to get a guy in free to the class Play and so I will write an Editorial saying that nobody be admitted for less than five dollars.

Yours Sin Searedly

Ernie Hemingway.

P. S. Please note that in this letter I have not referred to no guys but Savage and this is not because I ain't ascairt of Savage. But I do not think he will get sore because he is a friend of mine and sits by me in Commercialized Law.   E. H.

WHO'S WHO IN BEAU BRUMMEL?

———

**By Roland Michael Kenney and
Ernest Monahan Hemingway.**

Huxham (Mortimer): Noted octogenarian, honorary member of Borrowed Time club, regarded as one of the institutions of the school. Experienced lover. Favors war. Is too small for the army, known as "The Grand Old Man".

Ray Ohlsen (Footman): Experience in handling feet acquired by working in shoe department of Fields and as captain of soccer team made him logical choice for Prince's footman. Is member of firm of Cohan and Hemigstein.

Morris Musselman: (Beau) Born-Yes. Nationality — Presbyterian. Education — No. Favorite Flower—Ceresota. If nerve was Gaul Mussie would be Europe. Known as "The Richard Mansfield of the Ghetto." Pilots the Air Line and a Dodge. Favorite literature "Old Doc Yak". Known as Beau because he wore bows on his shoes and his trousers and tied his tie in a bow. Also came out afterward and made a bow. Otherwise did not look like a bo.

Dale Bumstead (Reginald): Makes love like Plato (a very high brow joke, ask your desk room teacher). Resembles Mussie as an actor in one respect—he also drives a Dodge. When he comes in the room in the last scene Beau sees him and drops dead. Draw your own conclusions.

Miss Dixon: The lady who took the play out of class play. Ask the cast.

Miss Hull: A violator of the 8 hour labor law for actors. Ask the dancers.

59

"BEAU BRUMMEL"

"Beau Brummel"

(By Clyde Fitch)

CAST

Beau Brummel	Morris Musselman
The Prince of Wales	Thomas Cusack
Richard Brinsley Sheridan	Ernest Hemingway
Lord Manly	Robert Cole
Reginald Courtenay	Dale Bumstead
Mortimer	Le Roy Huxham
Mr. Abrahams	Allen Speelman
Simpson	Julian Lull
Bailiffs	Harry King Lyman Worthington
Prince's Footman	Ray Ohlsen
Mr. Oliver Vincent	Lloyd Golder
Mariana Vincent	Dorothy Estabrook
Kathleen	Gladys Johnson
Duchess of Leamington	Elizabeth Wanzer
Lady Farthingale	Carroll Dyrenforth
French Lodging House Keeper	Olga Flohr
Mrs. St. Aubyn	Roberta Finnell

Other Ladies and Gentlemen—

Betty Brydon	Hillyard Gage
Ruth Morrison	Marshall Wilson
Helen Shepherd	Paul Porch
Caroline Bagley	

61

Clarence Bailey Savage: He slings the scenery around. A bachelor—Eats right and left handed.

L. Worthington: A bailiff.

H. King: Ditto. Good looking.

Tom Cusack (Prince of Wales): Called the Prince of Whales on account of his feet. Spoke English, French and Profanity in the show.

Ernest Hemingway.

Hemingstien felt queer before the play and acted as he felt. He gave his best to the development of the drama but knocked the class out of the class play. A noble character until his death. Epitaph: E. M. H. Gone in All Departments.

Lloyd Golder: A good actor. Not a bachelor. Genius in expressing ability acquired by working for American Express Co.

Bob Cole (Lord Manly): A good argument for prohibition.

Allan Speelman (Abrahams): A swell jew! We didn't know it was in him

Julian Lull, (Simpson;) Helen thinks he did finely. So do we.

Dorothy Estabrook (Mariana), Gladys Johnson (Kathleen), Elizabeth Wanzer (Dutchess), Carrol Dyrenforth (Lady Farthingale), Olga Flohr (F. L. H. Keeper), Roberta Finnell (Mrs. St. Aubyn): We're too bashful. Read what Sue says about them.

---

2 March 1917, 1 & 4

NEW TRIER TANKERS WIN FROM LOCALS

Oak Park Splashers Cop Close Water Basket Game.

By Ernest Hemingway.

For the second time this year the New Trier swimming team won a one sided meet from the Oak Park squad by the score of 44–15.

As usual Oak Park was without the services of their constantly ineligible stars and Standish joined the missing pair due to parental objection to his swimming.

Oak Park secured some revenue by defeating the crack New Trier water basket ball team in a close game 1–0.

The high school meet was staged in conjunction with a university meet between Northwestern and Wisconsin and a large crowd was present.

Schaeffer, the national interscholastic plunging champ, copped first honors in his event with a mark of 24 seconds for the sixty feet.

This time was 18 seconds faster than the time made in the university event and the Oak Park plungers were not in the running against him. Smeeth of Oak Park did excellent work in this event, his first appearance in the Senior plunge. Only one of the university plungers went 60 feet and all of the high school plungers went further than two of the college athletes.

Cap White of Oak Park took a third in the 40 yard swim and swam a fine race in the relay.

Brandt of Oak Park came in third in the 10 yard breast stroke, but was disqualified for not touching the rail with both hands. This was the first time Brandt had beaten his team mate Musselman in this event, but as Mussie was only a couple of inches behind the third place went to Oak Park anyway.

Uhlman, O. P., finished 3d in the 100 in a tight case and Hurst, O. P., garnered a 2d in the 60 yard back stroke.

In the fancy diving Herb Mills, of O. P., took first place and Ellis, O. P., copped second. Oak Park's fancy floppers far outclassed the New Trier divers.

New Trier team barely nosed out the Oak Park water cleavers in the relay.

At water basket ball Oak Park team composed of White, Royal, Musselman (forwards), Hurst, Ullman and Hemingway (guards) downed New Trier 1-0. Royal scored Oak Park's one ringer on a free throw. The New Trier team claimed the western interscholastic championship at this sport.

———————

OAK PARK TEAM WINS FROM MAIN HIGH

Team Cops First in All But Two Events.

TIE FAST WATER BASKET GAME

By Ernest Miller Hemingway

Maine High School's swimming aspirations were given a set back Saturday night when the Oak Park team humbled the Desplaines' squad by a count of 36-24.

In the water basket ball game that followed the meet the count was knotted at the finish 4-4.

For Oak Park Standish won individual honors with a first in the 100 yard swim, a third in the 40 and by swimming on the winning relay team.

As the meet was run off under the intercollegiate rules, the relay was the first event.

Oak Park put this event on ice with a team composed of Standish, Ellis, Uhlman and White. Next on the schedule was the fancy diving which was won by Mills of Oak Park with a big point margin. Ellis, his team mate, finished third.

Cowno of Maine took first honors in the forty yard swim with White and Standish finishing second and third.

Swimming in the 40 yard breast stroke, Bill Brandt finished second only a few inches behind the winner.

Oak Park also showed enough to take the major number of places in the plunge.

Ingalls of Oak Park placed second with a dive of 52 feet. Ingalls, who is a Freshman, is doing finely in this event and with three more years of competition before him ought to be an inter-scholastic champion by the time he finishes school.

Pete Chase took first in the 40 yard back stroke. Pete copped comfortably and Ellis took third in this event.

The crowd was in a continual uproar cheering the water basket ball game which was the hardest contest the Oak Park sextette has engaged in this year. It was featured by rough work on both sides and at the close the score was tied at 4 all. Mills dropped in both Oak Park's ringers.

O. P. PLACES SECOND IN SUBURBAN CLASSIC

Sutphen Shatters Record in 440.

O. P. RELAY TEAM SHOWS SUPERIORITY.

By Ernest Hemingway.

Results of meet.

Senior—University High 44, Oak Park 35, La Grange 33½, New Trier 16½, Evanston 3.

Junior—New Trier 29½. Evanston 10, La Grange 7, University High 5½, Oak Park 5.

By the close margin of only nine points U. High nosed out Oak Park for premier honors in the Suburban Interscholastic Saturday at Patten. Marvon prep. athletes captured first place in the Senior meet with 44 points. Oak Park came in second with 35 points and La Grange finished third with 33½ points.

In the Senior meet New Trier, the dark horse, came out on top with 29½ points, with Evanston and La Grange winning second and third.

Numerous Suburban indoor records were smashed by the competing athletes.

Chet Sutphen shattered Roberts' old record of 58 seconds in the 440 by traveling the distance in 53 3-g seconds.

Hoyne of U. High broke "Ev." Royal's shotput record of 41 feet 6½ inches by a heave of 48 feet 8 inches. Swezey of La Grange topped the former high jump record of 5 feet 5 inches by ⅜ of an inch.

Oak Park track men placed in every event but

67

the pole vault and shotput and won three events—the Senior 50-yard low hurdles, 440-yard run and Senior relay.

In the 50-yard dash Lockyer and Henkle got into the finals and Lockyer took a third in the final heat.

Blount placed second in the 50-yard high hurdles in a close race, beating both Kounovsky and Wilson of La Grange.

Oak Park grabbed first and fourth places in the 50-yard low hurdles. Savage leaped over the barriers in .06 4–5 for the first honors and Pentecost copped fourth place.

Standish placed third in the mile run against a big field. The tank man ran a fine race and finished just a couple of feet behind the winner.

Jack Lockyer ran the 220 in second best time and "Hox" King shared third place with two U. High men.

Westy Moore finished third in the 880 with Blount right behind him for fourth place.

In the record-breaking time of 53 3–5 seconds Sutphen broke the tape in the 440-yard run. Grimm of Oak Park ran a heady race and added a third to Oak Park's total.

Captain Pentecost garnered a second in the running broad jump. Jack was greatly handicapped in this event because he had been unable to practice due to bad weather outdoors.

Pentecost also tied Thomas of U. High for third in the running high jump.

Oak Park showed that it has the best relay team in the Suburban league by taking that race in a brilliant manner. All of the relay men ran well but King was the man that cinched the race by his wonderful driving finish.

The Junior track men gathered five points in their meet, Blount taking a third in the Junior low hurdles and a fourth in the shotput while the Junior relay team placed third in that race.

This Saturday Oak Park meets U. High in a dual meet and one of the best contests of the season is expected.

———————

THE TRAPEZE

Weekly News Organ
of the
Oak Park and River Forest
Township High Schoo.)

Our Motto:
The Best Is None Too
Good for Us.

VOL. VI. NO. 19   OAK PARK, ILL., FRIDAY, MARC...   PRICE 2 CENTS

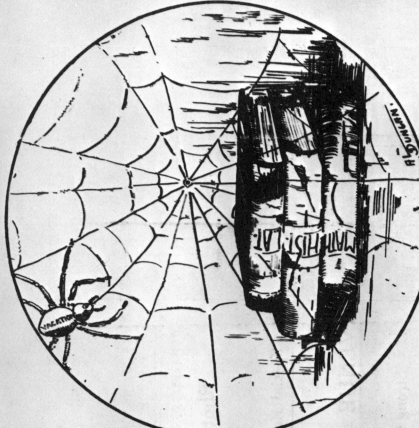

TRACK TEAM LOSES TO CULVER

Savage, Lockyer, Cole and Blount Individual Point Winners—Others Star.

OAK PARK STEADY TEAM

By Ernest Hemingway

Unable to give Culver any competition in the field events, Oak Park lost a track meet to the cadets 57½ to 34½. Oak Park was superior to the Culverites in the track events but the illness of Captain Pentecost and the absence of a weight man gave Culver a clean sweep in the pole vault, high jump and the first two places in the shot put.

Savage was the individual point winner for Oak Park with nine points taking a first in the 35 yd. high hurdles, a second in the low hurdles and a third in the shot.

Lockyer garnered a first in the dash and a second in the 220 for a total of eight points.

The feature race of the day was the mile which Sutphen captured with a time of 4:59 2-5, breaking the track record by eight seconds. Sutphen ran a brilliant race and sprinted the last three laps at 220 pace. His time is marvelous for the Culver track, which is an 18 lap parallel affair, greatly resembling a trough.

Cole took a second in the 35 yd. low hurdles and Blount the same place in the 35 yard highs.

In the furlong Seelyer placed second and Hox King split third place with a Culver man. Westy Moore grabbed secondary honors in the 880 yd. run and was the only Oak Parker to place.

Culver came out ahead in the relay by a six inch margin. All through the meet the orange and blue athletes were handicapped by inability to take the turns on the poor Culver track.

This afternoon Oak Park goes to Evanston for the preliminaries of the big Northwestern National Inter-

JUNIOR TRACK TEAM DEFEATS AUSTIN

Cup From City Rivals, Stresser Beaten in Sprints.

BLOUNT SETS RECORD OF 1:25.05 IN 600 YD. RUN

By Earl Pashley

Oak Park's junior track team defeated Austin last Tuesday in a closely contested meet in the field gymnasium by a sc...e to 52½ score. Stresser ... Austin proved to be the individual point winner, scoring six points. The Austin star took firsts in the 35 yd. low entries and three standing jumps and tied or second in the 220 yd. dash and high jump. Barnes of Austin copped second honors with eleven points.

Blount won the 600 yd. run as usual and established a track record, covering the distance in 1:25 flat. In this event only four men finished and all wore Orange and Blue. Osborne nosed out Standish for second place with Buckley of Oak Park finishing fourth. In a mixup on the fourth lap two of Austin's three entrants were jostled off the track and the remaining Austinite dropped out on account of the hot pace set by Blount.

Stresser of Austin, who finished second in the 50 yd. dash at Northwestern University interscholastic did not live up to expectations in the short sprint, both Barney and Godfrey of Oak Park and Barnes of Austin coming in ahead of him.

In the low hurdles Blount defeated Stresser in his heat but stumbled on the first hurdle in the finals and could not place. Osborne leaped farther than Stresser in the three jumps but fell back so his mark did not count. His next best jump gave him second place.

Hatchman of Austin was easily the class of the field in the shot put, heaving the egg at 35 ft. 2 in. This is the best mark ever made in a meet in Oak Park's gym. Radke copped

scholastic meet which will be run off tonight.

Tomorrow night the finals will be held and a big Oak Park delegation is expected to be on hand. The meets will be held in Patten gym and will start at 3 p. m. both Friday and Saturday night. Tickets may be obtained at the gym.

Summaries

25 yd. low hurdles: 1st, Savage, O. P.; 2d, Savage, O. P.; 3d, Cole, O. P.

35 yd. high hurdles: 1st, Savage, O. P.; 2d, Blount, O. P.; 3d, Clere, C.

35 yd. dash: 1st, Lockyer, C.; 2d, Murray, C.; 3d, Whitehead, C.

Mile run: 1st, Suphen, O. P.; 4:59 2-3; 2d, Cushing, C.; 3d, Goodell, O. P.

880 run: 1st, Whitehead, C., 2:20; 2d Moore, O. P.; 3d. Brown, C.

220 yd. dash: 1st, Murray, C., :27; 2d, Lockyer, O. P.; 3d, King, O. P. and Reefale, O. P.

High Jump: 1st, Payne, C., 5 ft. 7 in.; 2d, Wakefield, C.; 3d, Brady, C.

Shot put: 1st, Korkey, C., 41 ft. 3 in.; 2d, Balam, C.; 3d, Savage, O. P.

Relay won by Culver, time 1:30 4-5. Kieferle, Murray, Whitehead and Konkey.

HATCH TALKS AT ART CLUB

A stereopticon lecture on the English abbeys and cathedrals was given by Mr. Hatch to the Art club last Tuesday.

As Mr. Hatch has visited all of the places shown, his talk contained many personal notes about the various historical and romantic spots. Among the most interesting abbeys is Melrose, where, under the altar, are buried the remains of Robert Bruce, the most heroic of the Scottish kings.

Of the cathedrals, York and Lincoln are considered the most beautiful and picturesque while even the mere name of Canterbury Cathedral has the glamour that draws people still from "stronge strandes". It was there that Thomas a'Becket the "holy blissful martyr" of Chaucer's prologue, was slain before the altar of St. Benedict. It is also the comb of the Black Prince, or by name, Edward, Prince of Wales, Edward III's eldest son.

Mr. Hatch showed a few views of the noted English colleges and gave many facts concerning the styles of architecture in the abbeys and cathedrals of England.

Directly following the change in the Drama club requirements comes the announcement that the Junior girls will be given a chance to make the Story club. Heretofore the club held a short story writing contest for Sophomore girls every spring. This new rule gives girls one more opportunity to be a member. This year a contest for both Junior and Sophomore girls will be held some time in April.

WATER BASKETBALL NEW SPORT

Oak Park Shows Great Ability in Game. Makes Swimming Meets Exciting.

By. Wilbur Brandt.

Since the new tank at the Y. M. C. A. now contains facilities for regulation water basketball the Oak Park water basketball team, runner-up in the middle west championship, is now putting in some hard practice. As soon as the team rounds into better shape Manager Ellis plans to challenge the Evanston champions.

The game of water basketball is played under nearly the same rules as floor basketball. It is an exceedingly exciting and intense game to watch as there is quick and strenuous action every minute. The game requires much endurance and speed for the forwards and lots of scrap for the guards. Hemingway and Ulhman are the guards and have shown plenty of fight in the games. With the new spacious seating gallery a good crowd should be out to see the next game.

Oak Park meets Crane April 6 in a swimming and water basketball meet. The local splashers will be without two reliable men but expect little trouble with Crane as this school's showing in previous meets does not indicate a very strong squad and their times have not been equal to the times made by the Oak Park squad. This meet will probably close the swimming season for Oak Park so a large crowd ought to be on hand. It has been rumored that Manager Ellis has engaged the services of the famous school "jazz band" to liven things up.

HOLDS MEETING

Former Oak Park Students Praised—Scholarship High—Athletics and Junior High School Discussed.

ALLISON NOMINATED

The patrons of the Oak Park High School held their annual meeting last Monday evening and the usual business was conducted. President J. K. Ingalls read his report at this time.

Mr. Ingalls' report covered a large field. He referred to the scholarship records made by Oak Park students at the different colleges and universities. These have from time to time appeared in the columns of this paper. Reference was also made to the high grade of scholarship attained here by Oak Park students. From these two statements it can readily be seen that the good students here at High School usually make good students in the colleges and universities.

The extensive use of athletic equipment was given some attention. Oak Park is certainly very efficient in athletics, as has been demonstrated by the showing of our teams. This is largely due to the equipment furnished the school body with which to train. We have apparatus of which any high school should be proud while our new athletic field would be hard to beat.

A Junior High School was favored. Mr. Ingalls promised the support of the board in any undertaking along this line. The High School is becoming crowded and our enrollment is rapidly increasing with prospects of even larger growth in the near future. Some plan must be devised to meet this growth. So far the Junior High School is the only feasible plan offered. If put in operation the members of the eighth grades and the first year high school pupils would go to a special school built to meet their needs.

Mr. Allison, who has faithfully served a term as a member of the school board, has been nominated for re-election. He is the only member to be elected this year.

The annual letter writing contest staged by Lake Forest College will take place in a few weeks. A preliminary contest will be given in the high school and the winners will be sent to the real contest at Lake Forest.

Mr. Platt and the English teachers have selected the following Seniors to compete in the preliminary contest: Caroline Bagley, Edward Wilcox, Margaret Wright, Edith Ebersold, Esther Pomeroy, Marcelline Hemingway, Virginia Reid, Zelma Owen, Florence Winder, Arthur Thexton, Martha Whitlock.

PROM PLANS PROGRESSING

Some people insist the plans for the Junior Prom should be kept a secret but when so many good times are being suggested all at one time, why not tell some? We'll still have a few left for surprises.

Just at present the entertainment committee is more important than the others because the entertainment will be so different from any we have ever had before and this year the entertainment forms so large a part of the Prom. Moreover, to secure the talent desired, dates must be booked early. Of the several male quartets recommended which one would add the most jollity with harmony to the program? Of all the instruments that can be used ensemble for group numbers, which combination would be most acceptable? And of all the readings in the world (with a man at our disposal who can give any of them), what shall our choice be? It is evident that the committee has quite enough work for even its ability.

As for decorations, as many flags are needed as dollars. It will take more flags to cover that gym than silver dollars for the floor of the Palmer House barber shop. Everybody must be the Old Electroscope and smiler all the Old Glories that Oak Park and River Forest have. The committee in charge are: Roland Hurt and Helen Condron, chairmen. Ruth Barr, Dorothy Dungan, Margaret Kelley, Marion Simpson, Agnes Tough, Clarence Savage, Whitford Baldwin, Gordon Crawford, Roderick Grant, Stewart Standish, committee members.

second place with a put of 42 ft. Blount getting third with 41 ft. 9½.

Oak Park ran away with the relay, Stoddard, Oak Park's last man coming in half a lap ahead of Austin's runner. Quite a little excitement was caused in the relay when the Austin coach claimed that Radke did not touch Stoddard, but he finally gave in, cinching the meet for Oak Park.

Summary:

35 yd. dash: Harvey, O. P. 1st; Godfrey, O. P., 2d; Barnes, A., 3d; time 4 2-5 sec.

35 yd. low hurdles: Stresser, A. 1st; Barnes A., 2d; Radke, O. P., 3d; time 4 4-5 sec.

220 yd. dash: Barnes, A., 1st; Bodfrey, O. P., Stresser, A., and Harvey, O. P., tied for 2d; time 27 2-5 sec.

660 yd. run: Blount, O. P., 1st; Osborne, O. P., 2d; Standish, O. P., 3d; time 1:35 (record).

High jump: Lewis, O. P., 1st; Barnes and Stresser, A., tied for 2d; height 5 ft. 1 in.

2 standing jumps: Stresser, A. 1st; Osborne, O. P., 2d; Pencecost, O. P., 3d; distance 27 ft 5 in.

Shot put: Hatchman, A., 1st; Radke, O. P., 2d; Blount, O. P., 3d; distance 40 ft. 3 in.

880 yd. relay: won by Oak Park (Godfrey, Stoddard, Radke and Harvey); time 1:34:1.

CONTESTS AT U. OF CHICAGO

On April 13 a band of 18 Seniors will leave Oak Park to try their abilities in the Chicago University Scholarship Contest. Some very excellent talent is being sent down this year and Oak Park should come home with more than a few scholarships. This year tests must be taken in two subjects instead of one so an all-around scholar has a better chance. Those taking the examinations are:

Helen Cirese—English-History.
Edward Wagenknecht—Eng.-Hist.
Edward Wilcox—Latin-French.
Elizabeth Kimball—Latin-History.
Louise Lucas—Latin-English.
Pauline High—German-English.
Olga Flohr—German-English.
Margaret Reelman—Hist.-English.
Robert Cole—Math.-Physics.
Louis Albee—Mathematics-History.
Wayne Brandstadt—Math.-Science.
Margaret Wright—Math.-English.
Ester Pomeroy—Math.-English.
Dorothy Estabrook—Reading.
Le Roy Husher—Public Speaking.
Frank Reid—Public Speaking.

TRACK TEAM LOSES
TO CULVER

**Savage, Lockyer, Cole and Blount
Individual Point Winners—
Others Star.**

OAK PARK STEADY TEAM

By Ernest Hemingway

Unable to give Culver any competition in the field events, Oak Park lost a track meet to the cadets 57½ to 34½. Oak Park was superior to the Culverites in the track events but the illness of Captain Pentecost and the absence of a weight man gave Culver a clean sweep in the pole vault, high jump and the first two places in the shot put.

Savage was the individual point winner for Oak Park with nine points taking a first in the 35 yd. high hurdles, a second in the low hurdles and a third in the shot.

Lockyer garnered a first in the dash and a second in the 220 for a total of eight points

The feature race of the day was the mile which Sutphen captured with a time of 4:59 2–5, breaking the track record by eight seconds. Sutphen ran a brilliant race and sprinted the last three laps at 220 pace. His time is marvelous for the Culver track, which is an 18 lap parallel affair, greatly resembling a trough.

Cole took a second in the 35 yd. low hurdles and Blount the same place in the 35 yard highs.

In the furlong Seekyer placed second and Hox King split third place with a Culver man. Westy Moore grabbed secondary honors in the 880 yd. run and was the only Oak Parker to place.

Culver came out ahead in the relay by a six inch margin. All through the meet the orange and blue athletes were handicapped by inability to take the turns on the poor Culver track.

This afternoon Oak Park goes to Evanston for the preliminaries of the big Northwestern National Interscholastic meet which will be run off tonight.

Tomorrow night the finals will be held and a big Oak Park delegation is expected to be on hand. The meets will be held in Patten gym and will start at 8 p. m. both Friday and Saturday night. Tickets may be obtained at the gym.

Summaries

25 yd. low hurdles: 1st, Clere, C., :04:5; 2d, Savage, O. P.; 3d, Cole, O. P.

35 yd. high hurdles: 1st, Savage, O. P.; 2d, Blount, O. P.; 3d Clere, C.

35 yd. dash: 1st, Lockyer, O. P., :04; 2d, Murray, C.; 3d, Whitehead, C.

Mile run: 1st, Sutphen, O. P., 4:59 2-3; 2d, Cushing, C.; 3d, Goodell, C.

880 run: 1st, Whitehead, C., 2:20; 2d Moore, O. P.; 3d, Brown, C.

220 yd. dash: 1st, Murray, C., :27; 2d, Lockyer, O. P.; 3d, King, O. P. and Reefale, O. P.

High Jump: 1st, Payne, C., 5 ft. 7 in.; 2d, Wakefield, C.; 3d, Brady, C.

Shot put: 1st, Korkey, C., 41 ft. 3 in.; 2d, Balam, C.; 3d, Savage, O. P.

Relay won by Culver, time 1:30 4-5, Kieferle, Murray, Whitehead and Konkey.

THE TRAPEZE

Weekly News Organ
of the
Oak Park and River Forest
Township High School

Our Motto:
The Best Is None Too
Good for Us.

VOL. VI. NO. 20   OAK PARK, ILL., FRIDAY, APRIL 20, 1917.   PRICE 2 CENTS

OAK PARK WINS THREE BASEBALL GAMES

Thistlethwaite Pleased With Team's Showing in Early Games—Pitchers Show Class.

By R. Harry MacNamara

Oak Park's baseball team has jumped into the lead in the race for the Suburban league flag with three straight wins, Proviso, Deerfield and Morton being the victims. Coach Thistlethwaite seems to have produced a winner and the team is confident of the championship.

Few high school teams are fortunate in having two good pitchers at the same time but in Matthews and Magrath Oak Park has two of the best high school twirlers in Cook county. "Swede" Swanson has become a capable little back stop and is holding up the receiving end of the battery in a masterful style.

Fred Wilcoxen is performing at his old station, the initial sack, but is a much improved ball player, both in hitting and fielding. "Wally" Wilson, a recruit, is covering the keystone sack a la Collins and seems to be the find of the year because he is also able to sting the horsehide. Uteritz is stationed in the short field and although a wonderful little player last year, seems to have improved with the bat and his work with Wilson at second reminds one of the championship combination in 1915. Steger and Uteritz. Bob Cole is covering the hot corner in a capable manner.

Capt. Powers is at his old stand in left field and is putting up a grand fielding game, but is not hitting at his usual clip, however, the season is still young and with a little warm weather he will be up to his old tricks. "Bill" Phelps is still chasing them in center and the hitter who hits one out there wants to hit it hard because "Bill" can sure travel. "Willie" has improved wonderfully at the bat. Coach Thistlethwaite is having some trouble in selecting his right fields and has tried several men, Kendall, Aeum, Studdard, Fogel and Schwab all taking a turn. Kendall seems to

OAK PARK SECOND IN NORTHWESTERN U

Entire Year Has Been Successful— Girls Have Heard Good Programs

CULVER TAKES MEET

By Ernest Hemingway

Individual prowess by Clarence Savage, Jack Lockyer and Walter Blount brought Oak Park 9½ points in the Northwestern U. National Interscholastic and the work of the medley relay team which placed second and added enough points to give the Orange and blue team second place. They shared second honors with Cicero and La Grange, each team amassing 12½ points.

Culver Military Academy, with a well balanced team took the meet with a total of 37 points.

Savage was Oak Park's individual star, gathering a second in both the high and low hurdles. Lockyer placed second in the dash only a hair's breadth behind Doweling of Bowen.

Blount, who was doped to win the 660 yard run, was forced to start at the very end of a squad of about twenty runners but succeeded in passing all but two of them.

Oak Park's medley relay team, composed of Lockyer, King, Moore and Sutphen, ran an excellent race and copped second place. The medley team would have won handily but for the fact that Weston Moore was unable to put up his usual fine race due to an injury to his leg, which was hurt when he was tripped and had a bad spill in the qualifying heats Friday night.

Oak Park's indoor track team this season was handicapped ever since the first race by inability to put its full strength in the field due to the absence in the last two meets of Captain Pentecost due to sickness and the ineligibility of star athletes all during the season.

Prospects for an out door track championship are very brilliant as Pentecost is again out and the other missing athletes have made up their scholastic deficiencies. With all the talent out Oak Park will have the best

GIRLS CLUB HOLDS FINAL MEETING

MISS BARTELME LAST SPEAKER

By Helen Carr

Girls' club assembled last Wednesday afternoon to hear Miss Mary Bartelme, assistant to Judge Arnold of the juvenile court of Chicago. An unusually large audience came out to this last meeting of the year to hear the climax of a year's good programs.

Miss Bartelme thanked the girls for the spirit of sympathy and helpfulness which has expressed itself in action more than in words, since she last spoke in Oak Park. She mentioned especially the appreciation of the young girls who were sent across the lake last summer for a vacation, by funds given from Oak Park. To those who, living in Chicago, had never seen the lake, others whose greatest travel had been a street car ride, and the majority who had never seen three square meals appear on their home tables in succession, this experience was a wonderfully happy one.

These girls have never forgotten this great event in their lives and wonder if they will ever have anything like again.

The girls whose homes, for one reason or another, are unfit for them to remain there unless sent to the Juvenile Detention Home, are sent to the home maintained in Austin by Miss Bartelme. A little Italian girl whose drunken father doesn't want her at home unless she can bring home five dollars a week, a pretty little Greek girl deserted by her mother, tiny girls who have tried to die before anything worse could happen, are fair samples of those brought to the Home, to remain there temporarily, until homes can be found for them. But they forget the hard times under the kindly care of Miss Fritz and the helpful interest of Miss Bartelme. With Miss Fritz as the head of the home and in her Miss Bartelme is

The next league game is scheduled for next Saturday, when the Orange and Blue athletes will journey to New Trier where they hope to enact some vengeance for the basketball defeat. The team has not been supported as it should be and the students should show some spirit by coming out to the games. Help the boys by doing your share. Watch the study hall boards for the announcement of the next home game. Get together and boost a winner.

By Elwood Ratcliff

On account of the uncertain conditions into which the country has been thrown by being forced into war, there was some doubt in the minds of many parents, whether or not it would be better to give up the Junior Prom and give the money to the Red Cross work.

This was thought important enough for consideration on the part of the Seniors, and so a class meeting was called 3d period last Monday. After discussing the matter, two motions were carried, first, that the Seniors should accept the invitation of the Juniors, and second, that the Seniors should suggest that the expenses be cut down, so that some of the funds might be given to the Red Cross.

Tuesday the Junior Executive Committee formally accepted these motions, besides voting 14 to 3 to carry on the original plans. The Junior meeting was held Wednesday—third period, and by a standing vote, the class expressed its favor in accord with that of the committee. In doing so, it was felt that, as the plans had all been made before war was inevitable, it was no sign of a lack of patriotism. Then too, the Prom was planned to be much simpler than last year, when the Social Committee of members first started planning.

And so, with most of the pledges collected and the preparations gradually being made, the third year students have high hopes of giving the outgoing class a party which will do them honor.

FRENCH CLUB NEXT WEEK

Club meetings have again started out in earnest and French club will have an unusually attractive meeting next Wednesday afternoon. Good speakers and good eats are promised.

After a two weeks' vacation in the way of clubs, French club has again started up with all its former activities but with an added attraction for this next meeting. A good speaker is promised and although we are unable to state definitely who it is to be, Miss Ferris says he will be excellent. Further entertainment will be furnished by Miss Maude Hulbert, a former graduate of Oak Park, who will sing French songs.

Good eats are promised by the committee in charge. Tickets will be on sale next week. Everybody out.

GIRLS FROM 15 TO 19 ADMITTED

By Marcelline Hemingway

The most inspiring series of meetings ever held in Oak Park is to take place this week end under the name of the Oak Park Conference of Girls.

For several weeks a body of "key girls", one from each church and Camp Fire in the village, has been meeting with the promoters of the conference to plan for the time, place, and programs for this splendid event.

The Girls' Conference is a strictly high school affair, only girls from fifteen to nineteen years of age being admitted. The purpose of this conference is to bring together girls of all classes in the high school and to enthuse them with an ambition for leadership in the best things.

Not only have the most inspiring and enthusiastic speakers available been provided for the three days of conference, but a jolly good time, under the auspices of Miss Hull, has been arranged for Saturday afternoon on Mrs. Austin's lawn.

With a luncheon and banquet on Saturday also and a "Mothers' and Daughters' Tea" Sunday afternoon, the conference promises a social enjoyment never before experienced by such a large group of high school girls together.

Delegates from every Protestant church have been elected by their respective Sunday school classes and will attend every session of the conference including the social features. No adults, except the conference leaders will be admitted so the girls will feel that this is truly their own affair.

The first session of the conference is at 3 o'clock Friday afternoon. Saturday morning at 10 o'clock the second session begins, followed by luncheon. Games in the afternoon and the banquet at night. The evening session on Saturday is in charge of the Mrs. Raymond's class of the First Congregational church and promises to be a rousing one.

Sunday afternoon the last session

Continued on page 4.

Proviso

Oak Park journeyed to Proviso a week ago Thursday and while Ray Matthews administered the white wash his mates pounded out eleven hits and twelve runs. Matthews was very effective despite the cold and allowed but two hits and fanned seven.

Oak Park got away to a good start by scoring three runs in the first inning. Uteritz walked, Phelps bunted and both runners were safe. Both runners moved up on a short pass ball. Wilson fanned. Powers singled to short left, Uteritz and Phelps scoring. Powers stole second when Casey let his liner go through him. Wilcoxen fanned. Cole out, Meyer to Curtis—3 runs, 2 hits, 1 error.

In the third, the Orange and Blue athletes put the game on ice when hits by Phelps, Wilson, Rehm and Wilcoxen, added by errors by Casey and Bullard, netted five runs. Proviso was helpless before Matthews' slants and was no match for Thistelwaite's hustling crew. The final score was 12-0.

Deerfield

Last Saturday morning Deerfield's baseball hopes invaded Oak Park and Oak Park wrecked their hope by administering a 6-2 defeat.

Leonard Magrath took the hill for Oak Park and was opposed by a large blonde named Larson. Both hurlers got away well and neither side was able to score during the first three innings, but in the fourth inning Oak Park started something.

Capt. Powers got a life on Friebley's error, Kendall fanned, Wilcoxen singled over short. Both runners moved upon a short pass ball. Cole fouled out to Carlson. Swanson was safe and Powers scored when Holmes muffed his drive in deep center. Wilcoxen holding at third. Magrath walked, filling the bases. After working the count two and two Uteritz smashed a double between left and

Continued on page 4.

shape and it is very probable the Suburban outdoor interscholastic will be held here.

In the Beloit meet on May 5th, Oak Park will enter a team and also in the Lake Forest interscholastic, May 12, and the big Illinois interscholastic, May 19.

STUDENTS SUFFER WITH PARENTS IN THEIR BEREAVEMENT

We feel now a little of the sadness that war brings to a country in the injury and death of some of us.

Shortly after noon Tuesday an automobile carrying Arthur Sanders, aged 17, William Keedy, and William Pauson, both 16 years old, collided with an east bound Lake street car near William street, River Forest. William Pauson died immediately and William Keedy soon after reaching the hospital. Arthur Sanders is at the West Suburban hospital and according to the latest reports will live.

A feeling of sorrow settled upon the school. The seriousness of the situation was impressed upon all. It was difficult to realize that the accident had really happened. Our sympathies went out immediately to the members of the bereaved families. The school to some extent feels the same loss. We knew them on Monday; on Tuesday they were gone and all that was left was a feeling of vacancy. We can in no way show or express our regret for this sudden loss. We can only stand by and mourn.

Assembly Today.

Just as The Trapeze goes to press, word is received that the Assembly Speaker will be Rev. Ernest Wray Oneal of Joliet.

OPERA TICKETS ON SALE
NEXT WEDNESDAY, APRIL 25

---

have. The home is in a neighborhood where they see a great many automobiles, and the children often sigh for a ride. Any one who would like to give it to them would be most welcome.

Other aids mentioned by Miss Bartelme can be given to her through Miss Rattray and Miss Chamberlain. While waiting for Miss Bartime to arrive, the club was entertained by Marion Roberts and Helen Knudsen, who gave piano solos.

STORY CLUB OPEN TO JUNIOR AND SOPHOMORE GIRLS

LAST MEETING INTERESTING

By Florence Winder

This year the Story club will open its portals to both Junior and Sophomore girls in the annual contest which will begin immediately and will close at 2:45, May 18.

In previous years only Sophomores have had the opportunity to enter, thus giving a two years' membership, but this year the club has decided to take in a few more Juniors. This decision was made at the April meetings which was held at Miss Wright's.

The following stories were read: "Billy Forgot" by Helen Carr, "Shot by Whom?" by Florence Winder, and "The Awakening" by Rita Hebert. The conditions of the contest are as follows:

1. All stories must be original with the person presenting them and must be what is generally known as a short story—not a condensed novel or a character sketch.

2. They are to be marked with a fictitious name and to have affixed to them a sealed envelope containing the real name of the author and marked with the fictitious name and rank of the competitor.

3. Each story is to be written on uniform paper or paper of equivalent size in ink (or type written). The legibility of the writing is an important factor.

4. Each story to be submitted must be approved by some English teacher as to its characteristics, as a short story, legibility and neatness.

The stories will be collected from the English teachers at the close of school on May 18, judged, and the names of those accepted posted on the study hall board as soon as possible. Stories not accepted will be destroyed immediately without opening the names

OAK PARK SECOND IN NORTHWESTERN U

CULVER TAKES MEET

By Ernest Hemingway

Individual prowess by Clarence Savage, Jack Lockyer and Walter Blount brought Oak Park 9½ points in the Northwestern U. National Interscholastic and the work of the medley relay team which placed second added enough points to give the Orange and Blue team second place. They shared second honors with Cicero and La Grange, each team amassing 12½ points.

Culver Military Academy, with a well balanced team took the meet with a total of 37 points.

Savage was Oak Park's individual star, gathering a second in both the high and low hurdles. Lockyer placed second in the dash only a hair's breadth behind Doweling of Bowen.

Blount, who was doped to win the 660 yard run, was forced to start at the very end of a squad of about twenty runners but succeeded in passing all but two of them.

Oak Park's medley relay team, composed of Lockyer, King, Moore and Sutphen, ran an excellent race and copped second place. The medley team would have won handily but for the fact that Weston Moore was unable to put up his usual fine race, due to an injury to his leg, which was hurt when he was tripped and had a bad spill in the qualifying heats Friday night.

Oak Park's indoor track team this season was handicapped ever since the first race by inability to put its full strength in the field due to the absence in the last two meets of Captain Pentecost due to sickness and the ineligibility of star athletes all during the season.

Prospects for an out door track championship are very brilliant as Pentecost is again out and the other missing athletes have made up their scholastic deficiencies. With all their talent out Oak Park will have the best team in the Surburban League.

The track at the new field is in fine shape and it is very probable the Suburban outdoor interscholastic will be held here.

In the Beliot meet on May 5th, Oak Park will enter a team and also in the Lake Forest interscholastic, May 12, and the big Illinois interscholastic, May 19.

WIN TWO—LOSE ONE

———

New Trier and Crane Trounced

———

MAGRATH HURLS 2 HIT GAME

———

By Ernest Hemingway.

Oak Park has won two games and lost one since April 21st, defeating New Trier and Crane and dropping a close tilt to Senn.

Mathews held New Trier to four hits April 21st while his teammates were pounding Pattison of New Trier for eleven bingles and ten runs. The final score was 10 to 4 in favor of the Orange and Blue nine.

Crane fell victims to Thistlewaite's machine on last Wednesday by a 1–0 count. Len McGrath hurled the pellet and was touched for but two safe swats. Phelps was the hero of the contest, lacing the horse hide for three sacks in the fourth inning and then scoring on Wilson's slam. This victory avenged the defeat Oak Park suffered at the hands of Crane in the first game of the season.

The local squad lost a tight contest to Senn last Saturday, 4–1. Senn scored three runs in the ninth, breaking the knotted count and winning the game. Matthews hurled in good form and was knocked for only three safeties. Oak Park knocked out four safe swats but Noeller of Senn kept the hits scattered.

———

RING LARDNER RETURNS

Dear Marce:—

They tell me subscriptions and advertising has both fell off something immense since I writ one of these letters last and so as I ain't very busy I might as well try and put some of what Mussy calls the good old Jazz into the publication again.

But do not think I am stuck on myself because that is not so as you must of knew, living right in the same house with me all these years. Is it not so, Marcelline?

Well, there is not much to tell about now because there is not much doing only the Prom and C. Bailey Savage ast me to write on it so I won't. But C. Bailey had charge of the lights and done it in a good manner. (advt.)

Say, Marcelline, did you know that there is 5 pairs of brothers and sisters in school and invariabsolutely it is a strange coincidence that the sister is good looking and the brother is not? Schwabs, Shepherds, Condrons and Kafts and Hemingways, is it not most peculiar that except in one family the sister is an awful lot better looking than the brother. But we are too modest to say which family is the exception. Huh? Marce?

Now don't get sore and cut that out of the paper because you ain't got no proof I meant our family, and you know what "Blight" Wilcoxen says, "They can't can you if they ain't got nothing on you."

The Trapeze is short of stuff and so don't get sore if I string this out because anyway you should give me lots of space because we are sisters and brothers.

Poor P. White has got the chicken pox and

79

couldn't go to the Prom. He probably won't die but I thot, gosh, what if he should? So I writ an epitaph for him and it is a—(I'm afraid this must go).

"In bed we laugh, in bed we cry,
    In bed we live, in bed we die;
When to the Prom the students flocks
    P's home in bed—with chicken pox.

It is a good thing P. White has chicken pox instead of measles, because there ain't nothing what rhymes with measles only squeazles and how could a guy use squeazles in a epitaph?

When a guy is hard up for copy it is a swell stall to run some personals so here is some of the same;

Pure Personals

Miss Biggs gave a Senior Prom Friday night. Several couples attended the charming affair. A pleasant time was had by all who were present who united in expressing what a fine time they all had each and every one severally.

Modern Heroes: Mr. Evans.

The "Round Table Club" were entertained at "cards" by Mr. Frederick Stewart Wilcoxen Saturday night. The genial host loaned us car fare home.

A unique and unparalleled event occurred last Friday at 3 p. m. Royal Harry McNamara loaned us 1 dollar. Mr. McNamara still has hopes.

Stew Standish purchased a fresh strawberry short cake shortly after 5 p. m. last Monday at Oak's. Mr. Standish paid for the short cake with his own money. Mrs. Osbourne has recovered from the shock and is doing finely.

Mr. Lewis O. Clarahan, '15, returned from Illinois U. Saturday night and on Monday Mr. Clarahan demonstrated to us the overwhelming superiority of 4 aces over a full house. Mr. Clarahan refused to loan us car fare.

80

Monday Mr. Larson's class had a test in commercial law. Mr. Morris Musselman, known as the Bo of Bumville, remained at home suffering from an acute head ache.

Proctor S. Gilbert, '16, has decided to economize during the war and so during the duration of the awful conflict Mr. Gilbert will roll his own. As a further measure of economy Mr. Gilbert will borrow the makin's.

Well, Marce, I had better quit now but if you and Mr. Gehlman let this go thru you will be glad because think of the joy it may bring to some suffering heart.

"Lovingly?"

"Ernie"

P. S. I knowed you didn't want any hard guys in this, Marce, so I left out Jack Landers and "Percy Burke".

---

11 May 1917, 3

OAK PARK ATHLETES WIN BELOIT MEET

Cop Honors from Big Field—Show a Well Balanced Squad.

LOCKYER WINS THREE FIRSTS

By Ernest Hemingway.

Competing against twenty-five schools and 135 other athletes Oak Park won the Beloit College Interscholastic track meet with a score of 34 points Armstrong's men placed in every event but the pole vault, low hurdles and jumps and were eleven points ahead of East Aurora, which came in second with 23 points.

Jack Lockyer, Oak Park's lightning dash man, was individual honor winner with three firsts, taking the 50, 100, and 220 yard dashes and humbling the much touted Dowding of Bowen, who was forced into second place.

Savage showed his versatility as an all round athlete by placing in four different events. C. Bailey gathered thirds in the shot, discus, javelin and high hurdles.

Standish, the aquatic miler, grabbed a third place in his event by a game finish and added another marker to Oak Park's point column.

Chetter Sutphen, who was the favorite for first honors in the 440, was not entirely able to offset the lead that Reese of East Aurora got on the start but cut it down to a fraction of an inch and gave Oak Park a second.

In the 880 Wallie Blount came up from behind

in a hair raising finish and passed all but the fleet-
ing Reese at the finish

With Lockyer in first place at the finish of the
220 Hox King was right behind him and the first
and second places gave Oak Park eight points toward the final victory.

Captain Pentecost was not in his usual fine
form in the jumps but showed his class by his
sterling race in the relay, which was won by 30
yards due to the sprinting ability of Sutphen,
Pentecost, Lockyer and King. The relay team
absolutely outclassed its competitors and was
one of the sensations of the meet.

After the meet the relay team was filmed by a
prominent movie company with Cap Pentecost
holding the big silver cup.

In addition to the relay cup Oak Park was
presented with a large shield emblematic of their
victory.

The track coach of Beloit said that Oak Park
had the best balanced team that had ever won
premier honors at the Beloit classic.

This Saturday Oak Park has entered a team in
the big Lake Forest Interscholastic which is regarded as one of the biggest outdoor meets of the
season.

———————

SHOTGUN CLUB NEWS

Leroy Huxham, secretary of the Shotgun club, wishes to announce that the article in last week's edition stating that Fred Wilcoxen and Ernest Hemingway tied for first honors for the season's average was a mistake. An error was made in adding the totals and it was afterward found that Earle Pashley and Fred Wilcoxen were tied for the lead in the final footing of the season's averages.

In the shoot-off held this week Pashley won out and stands at the head of the list for the year 1917. The gun club is an independent organization composed of High School boys and is not in any way connected with the school. The club held its final meeting Monday night and has formally disbanded for the year.

H. E.

Attributed to Hemingway by Hanneman—C29₂.

SOME SPACE FILLED BY ERNEST MACNAMARA HEMINGWAY

Ring Lardner Has Objected to the Use of His Name.

Personal

Mr. Arthur Alonzo Thexton, known as the Smiling Blond Beauty, wishes to announce that his picture was not taken with the Hannah club or Girls' Rifle club. Mr. Thexton paid his 20c, however, and joined the French and Math clubs for pictorial purposes. Being unable to procure a suit, he was not filmed with the cadets.

George Washington

When we heard at the end of the first semester that a fellow by the name of George Washington had entered school we determined to look him up. Sutphen pointed him out and the following conversation (actual) took place.

We, "Hello Washington."

G. W., "Hello."

We, "Where you going"

G. W., "Over to baseball practice."

We, "What do you play?"

G. W., "Oh I'm a good pitcher and a pretty fair catcher and I can play second base right up along with all the rest of 'em."

We, "You don't need to practice. Going to try for the team?"

G. W., "Oh, I don't think I'll have to try very much. Where are you going?"

We, "Downtown to swim."

G. W., "I'm a good swimmer."

We, "What stroke do you swim?"

G. W., "What do you mean, stroke?"

We, "Do you swim the crawl?"

G. W., "Are you trying to kid me? I swim regular way, on my side."

We, "Oh!"

G. W., "What do you do?"

We, "I try to plunge."

G. W., "What's that."

We, "See how far you can dive."

G. W., "How far can you dive."

We, "Oh, about 100 yards." (World's record is 83 feet.)

G. W., "I can plunge about 75 yards." (Modestly.)

We, "That's great! Come on out for the team. You could get a place second or third any way."

G. W., "Sure if I get time. Where do you swim."

Us, "At Hamilton club."

G. W., "Can anybody swim there?"

We, "Sure It's kind of a public bath."

G. W., "I don't believe in Baths except on Saturday night. Who is that fellow."

Us, "That's Wilcoxen."

G. W., "Who's he?"

Us, "He's the assistant Principal."

G. W., "I'd like to meet him. Say, what's your name?"

We, "My name's McDaniel. I'm the Principal's son."

G. W., "You look a lot like him."

We, "Thank you George! Dad will be glad when I tell him that."

G. W., "Well, so long Macdaniels."

We, "So long George old man. Call me Mac. See you again soon."

And two days after just when that fertile field had opened up before us, G. W. had to quit school.

We met another interesting guy the other day

86

who had even a better line than the namesake of the father of our country. The conversation will be printed in the issue after next of the Trapeze. —advt.

Get your copies early.

The Ring Lardner for next week will be run by Stewart W. Standish, one of the most brilliant of the Juniors. We have known Stewart from childhood and feel deeply at seeing him come to this untimely end. The Trapeze extends thru this column its sympathies to the bereaved parents of this unfortunate youth who is so soon to fall in all the youthful vigor of his young manhood.

His mental loss will be ill able to be born by this community of which he was so promising a member.

HIGH LIGHTS AND
LOW LIGHTS

By Ernest Michealowitch Hemingway, B. S.

Mr. Dale Bumstead gives a dinner dance to-morrow night at the Country club. Messrs Morris Musselman, Fred Wilcoxen, Julius Caesar, Ray Ohlsen, Harry King, Ernest Hemingway, Abra-ham Lincoln and General Joffre will not be among those present, all having perfect alibis.

* * * *

The Trapeze extends its sympathy to the school over the prospective loss of LeRoy Huxham, who has been a familiar landmark for the last decade. Mr. Huxham's place will be almost impossible to fill but R. Harry McNamara will do, as the slangsters have, his "drundest."

* * * *

There is no book review in this week's Trapeze as Arthur A. Thexton was unable to procure a copy of Mr. Horatio Alger's latest masterpiece.

* * * *

Mr. Edward Wagenknecht gave an oration be-fore the 19th Century Civics club Saturday afternoon on "Where Is My Keeper?"

* * * *

Several members of the Trap Shooting club are exhibiting pieces of silver ware of the Ohl-sen's home as trophies of the meeting held there Wednesday night. The silverware is always the last stakes that Ray puts up.

*   *   *   *

The Oak Park Incompatable Cadet Corps have had model 1849 special muzzle loading rifles issued to them. Captain Porch says these are the rifles which won the war of 1812.

*   *   *   *

A new party enters the race next fall in the person of the anti prohibition party. Its leaders, led by Tom Cusack, nominated the modest editor of these columns and announced their slogan as "Hemingway and a full Stein!"

*   *   *   *

Mr. Walter Earle Pashley wishes to announce through these columns that the reason the price of the Examiner was raised to two cents was not solely because he was writing for it.

*   *   *   *

It is rumored that Mr. Charles A. Evans stood on his head at the Faculty picnic. Surely, as Shakespeare saith, "There is something that sticketh closer than a brother."

*   *   *   *

Mr. Richard Pentecost, one of the most active members of the younger set, has given up eating sundaes since the recent rise in price, none of Mr. Pentecost's friends being able to loan him 15 cents.

*   *   *   *

Miss Dorothy Estabrook wishes to announce that the picture used as an advertisement for the Drama club show was not a snap shot.

*   *   *   *

Miss Marcelline Hemingway, well known as the sister of the noted writer, has been faithfully practicing her commencement oration. Since the inauguration of these rehearsals we have haunted the office of the Oak Park Events.

* * * *

Knowing it will be a novel experience to them we would enjoy having the following people see their names in print
  C. Bailey Savage
  F. Stewart Wilcoxen
  Annette DeVoe
  Gordon Shepherd
  Katherine Meyer
  Mick Kenney

* * * *

Notice is hereby given all those to whom we owe money that whereas if Oak Park wins the Suburban League meet Saturday, you will all be promptly paid on presenting satisfactory evidences of debt.

* * * *

Mr. Larson entertained the Seventh Period Commercial Law Class at a slumber party last Tuesday.

* * * *

As a final low light this column will be closed with the following verse which we always write in memory books. Girls, cut it out and it will save you and us both trouble.
  'I've never guzzled beer nor wine,
  And yet they call me Heming "Stein"!
  Yours sincerely,
      (Cut this out too and S. U. B. C.)
  ERNEST McDERMOTT HEMINGWAY.

90

Photo courtesy W. Jones.

Oak Park, 1919.

91

The Tabula

TABULA

Vol XXIII   Oak Park, Ill., November, 1916   No. 1

XXII (February 1916), 9–10

JUDGMENT OF MANITOU

By Ernest Hemingway, '17

DICK HAYWOOD buttoned the collar of his mackinaw up about his ears, took down his rifle from the deer horns above the fireplace of the cabin and pulled on his heavy fur mittens. "I'll go and run that line toward Loon River, Pierre," he said. "Holy quill pigs, but it's cold." He glanced at the thermometer. "Forty-two below! Well, so long, Pierre." Pierre merely grunted, as, twisting on his snowshoes, Dick started out over the crust with the swinging snowshoe stride of the traveler of the barren grounds.

In the doorway of the cabin Pierre stood looking after Dick as he swung along. He grinned evilly to himself, "De tief will tink it a blame sight cooler when he swingin' by one leg in the air like Wah-boy, the rabbit; he would steal my money, would he!" Pierre slammed the heavy door shut, threw some wood on the fire and crawled into his bunk.

At Dick Haywood strode along he talked to himself as to the travellers of the "silent places." "Wonder why Pierre is so grouchy just because he lost that money? Bet he just misplaced it somewhere. All he does now is to grunt like a surly pig and every once in a while I catch him leering at me behind my back. If he thinks I stole his money why don't he say so and have it out with me! Why, he used to be so cheerful and jolly; when we agreed at Missainabal to be pardners and trap up here in the Ungava district, I thought he'd be a jolly good companion, but now he hasn't spoken to me for the last week, except to grunt or swear in that Cree lingo."

It was a cold day, but it was the dry, invigorating cold of the northland and Dick enjoyed the crisp air. He was a good traveller on snowshoes and rapidly covered the first five miles of the trap line, but somehow he felt that something was following him and he glanced around several times only to be disappointed each time. "I guess it's only the Kootzie-ootzie," he muttered to himself, for in the North whenever men do not understand a thing they blame it on the "little bad god of the Crees." Suddenly, as Dick entered a growth of spruce, he was jerked off his feet, high into the air. When his head had cleared

96

from the bang it had received by striking the icy crust, he saw that he was suspended in the air by a rope which was attached to a spruce tree, which had been bent over to form the spring for a snare, such as is used to capture rabbits. His fingers barely touched the crust, and as he struggled and the cord grew tighter on his led he saw what he had sensed to be following him. Slowly out of the woods trotted a band of gaunt, white, hungry timber wolves, and squatted on their haunches in a circle round him.

Back in the cabin Pierre as he lay in his bunk was awakened by a gnawing sound overhead, and idly looking up at the rafter he saw a red squirrel busily gnawing away at the leather of his lost wallet. He thought of the trap he had set for Dick, and springing from his bunk he seized his rifle, and coatless and gloveless ran madly out along the trail. After a gasping, breathless, choking run he came upon the spruce grove. Two ravens left off picking at the shapeless something that had once been Dick Haywood, and flapped lazily into a neighboring spruce. All over the bloody snow were the tracks of My-in-gau, the timber wolf.

As he took a step forward Pierre felt the clanking grip of the toother bear trap, that Dick had come to tend, close on his feet. He fell forward, and as he lay on the snow he said, "It is the judgment of Manitou; I will save My-in-gau, the wolf, the trouble."

And he reached for the rifle.

XXII (April 1916), 16–17

A MATTER OF COLOUR

By Ernest Hemingway

WHAT, you never heard the story about Joe Gan's first fight?" said old Bob Armstrong, as he tugged at one of his gloves.

"Well, son, that kid I was just giving the lesson to reminded me of the Big Swede that gummed the best frame-up we ever almost pulled off.

"The yarn's a classic now; but I'll give it to you just as it happened.

"Along back in 1902 I was managing a sort of a new lightweight by the name of Montana Dan Morgan. Well, this Dan person was one of those rough and ready lads, game and all that, but with no footwork, but with a kick like a mule in his right fin, but with a weak left that wouldn't dent melted butter. I'd gotten along pretty well with the bird, and we'd collected sundry shekels fighting dockwallopers and stevedores and preliminary boys out at the old Olympic club.

"Dan was getting to be quite a sizable scrapper, and by using his strong right mitt and stalling along, he managed to achieve quite a reputation. So I matched the lad with Jim O'Rourke, the old trial horse, and the boy managed to hang one on Jim's jaw that was good for the ten-second anesthetic.

"So when Pete McCarthy came around one day and said he had an amateur that wanted to break in, and would I sign Dan up with him for twenty rounds out at Vernon, I fell for it strong. Joe Gans, Pete said, was the amateur's name, and I'd never heard of him at that time.

"I thought that it was kind of strange when Pete came around with a contract that had a $500 forfeit clause in it for non-appearance, but we intended to appear all right, so I signed up.

"Well, we didn't train much for the scrap, and two days before it was to come off, Dan comes up to me and says: 'Bob, take a look at this hand.'

"He stuck out his right mauler, and there, just above the wrist, was a lump like a pigeon egg.

" 'Holy smokes! Danny, where did you get that?'

" 'The bag busted loose while I was punchin' it,' says Danny, 'and me right banged into the framework.'

" 'Well, you've done it now,' I

yelped. 'There's that 500 iron men in the forfeit, and I've put down everything I've got on you to win by K. O.'

" 'It can't be helped,' says Dan. 'That bag wasn't fastened proper; I'll fight anyway.'

" 'Yes, you will, with that left hand of yours, that couldn't punch a ripple in a bowl of soup.'

" 'Bob,' says Danny, 'I've got a scheme. You know the way the ring is out there at the Olympic? Up on the stage with that old cloth drop curtain in back? Well, in the first round, before they find out about this bad flipper of mine, I'll rush the smoke up against the curtain (you know Joe Gans was a "pusson of color") and you have somebody back there with a baseball bat, and swat him on the head from behind the curtain.'

"Say! I could have thrown a fit. It was so blame simple. We just couldn't lose, you see. It comes off so quick nobody gets wise. Then we collects and beats it!

"So I goes out and pawns my watch to put another twenty down on Dan to win by a knockout. Then we went out to Vernon and I hired a big husky Swede to do the slap-stick act.

"The day of the fight dawned bright and clear, as the sporting writers say, only it was foggy. I installed the husky Swede back of the old drop curtain just behind the ropes. You see, I had every cent we had down on Dan, about 600 round ones and the 500 in the forfeit. A couple of ham and egg fighters mauled each other in the prelims, and then the bell rings for our show.

"I tied Dan's gloves on, gives him a chew of gum and my blessing, and he climbs over the ropes into the squared circle. This Joe Gans, he's champion now, had quite a big following among the Oakland gang, and so we had no very great trouble getting our money covered. Joe's black, you know, and the Swede behind the scenes had his instructions: 'Just as soon as the white man backs the black man up against the ropes, you swing on the black man's head with the bat from behind the curtain.'

"Well, the gong clangs and Dan rushes the smoke up against the ropes, according to instructions.

"Nothing doing from behind the curtain! I motioned wildly at the Swede looking out through the peephole.

"Then Joe Gans rushes Dan up against the ropes. Whunk! comes a crack and Dan drops like a poled over ox.

"Holy smoke! The Swede had hit the wrong man! All our kale was gone! I climbed into the ring, grabbed Dan and dragged him into the dressing room by the feet. There wasn't any need for the referee to count ten; he might have counted 300.

"There was the Swede.

"I lit into him: 'You miserable apology for a low-grade imbecile! You evidence of God's carelessness! Why in the name of the Prophet did you hit the white man instead of the black man?'

"'Mister Armstrong,' he says, 'you no should talk at me like that —I bane color blind!'"

XXIII (November 1916), 8–9

SEPI JINGAN

By Ernest Hemingway, '17

" 'VELVET'S' like red hot pepper; 'P. A.' like cornsilk. Give me a package of 'Peerless'."

Billy Tabeshaw, long, lean, copper-colored, hamfaced and Ojibway, spun a Canadian quarter onto the counter of the little northwoods country store and stood waiting for the clerk to get his change from the till under the notion counter.

"Hey, you robber!" yelled the clerk. "Come back here!"

We all had a glimpse of a big, wolfish-looking, husky dog vanishing through the door with a string of frankfurter sausages bobbing, snake-like, behind him.

"Darn that blasted cur! Them sausages are on you, Bill."

"Don't cuss the dog. I'll stand for the meat. What's it set me back?"

"Just twenty-nine cents, Bill. There was three pounds of 'em at ten cents, but I et one of 'em myself."

"Here's thirty cents. Go buy yourself a picture post-card."

Bill's dusky face cracked across in a white-toothed grin. He put his package of tobacco under his arm and slouched out of the store. At the door he crooked a finger at me and I followed him out into the cool twilight of the summer evening.

At the far end of the wide porch three pipes glowed in the dusk.

"Ish," said Bill, "they're smoking 'Stag!' It smells like dried apricots. Me for 'Peerless.' "

Bill is not the redskin of the popular magazine. He never says "ugh." I have yet to hear him grunt or speak of the Great White Father at Washington. His chief interests are the various brands of tobacco and his big dog, "Sepi Jingan."

We strolled off down the road. A little way ahead, through the gathering darkness, we could see a blurred figure. A whiff of smoke reached Bill's nostrils. "Gol, that guy is smoking 'Giant'! No, it's 'Honest Scrap'! Just like burnt rubber hose. Me for 'Peerless.' "

The edge of the full moon showed above the hill to the east. To our right was a grassy bank. "Let's sit down," Bill said. "Did I ever tell you about Sepi Jingan?"

101

"Like to hear it," I replied.

"You remember Paul Black Bird?"

"The new fellow who got drunk last fourth of July and went to sleep on the Pere Marquette tracks?"

"Yes. He was a bad Indian. Up on the upper peninsula he couldn't get drunk. He used to drink all day —everything. But he couldn't get drunk. Then he would go crazy; but he wasn't drunk. He was crazy because he couldn't get drunk.

"Paul was Jack-fishing [spearing fish illegally] over on Witch Lake up on the upper, and John Brandar, who was game warden, went over to pinch him. John always did a job like that alone; so next day, when he didn't show up, his wife sent me over to look for him. I found him, all right. He was lying at the end of the portage, all spread out, face down and a pike-pole stuck through his back.

"They raised a big fuss and the sheriff hunted all over for Paul; but there never was a white man yet could catch an Indian in the Indian's own country.

"But with me, it was quite different. You see, John Brandar was my cousin.

"I took Sepi, who was just a pup then, and we trailed him (that was two years ago). We trailed him to the Soo, lost the trail, picked it up at Garden River, in Ontario; followed him along the north shore to Michipicoten; and then he went up to Missainabie and 'way up to Moose Factory. We were always just behind him, but we never could catch up. He doubled back by the Abittibi and finally thought he'd ditched us. He came down to this country from Mackinaw.

"We trailed him, though, but lost the scent and just happened to hit this place. We didn't know he was here, but he had us spotted.

"Last fourth of July I was walking by the P. M. tracks with Sepi when something hit me alongside the head and everything went black.

"When I came to, there was Paul Black Bird standing over me with a pike-pole and grinning at me!

" 'Well,' he smiled, 'you have caught up with me; ain't you glad to see me?'

"There was where he made a mistake. He should have killed me then and everything would have been all right for him. He would have, if he had been either drunk or sober, but he had been drinking and was crazy. That was what saved me.

"He kept prodding me with the pike-pole and kidding me. 'Where's your dog, dog man? You and he have followed me. I will kill you both and then slide you onto the rails.'

"All the time I kept wondering where Sepi was. Finally I saw him. He was crawling with his belly on the earth, toward Black Bird.

Nearer and nearer he crawled and I prayed that Paul wouldn't see him.

"Paul sat there, cussing and pricking me with the long pikepole. Sepi crawled closer and closer. I watched him out of the tail of my eye while I looked at Paul.

"Suddenly Sepi sprang like a shaggy thunderbolt. With a side snap of his head, his long, wolf jaws caught the throat.

"It was really a very neat job, considering. The Pere Marquette Resort Limited removed all the traces. So, you see, when you said that Paul Black Bird was drunk and lay down on the Pere Marquette tracks you weren't quite right. That Indian couldn't get drunk. He only got crazy on drink.

"That's why you and me are sittin' here, lookin' at the moon, and my debts are paid and I let Sepi steal sausages at Hauley's store.

"Funny, ain't it?

"You take my advice and stay off that 'Tuxedo'—'Peerless' is the only tobacco.

"Come on, Sepi."

XXIII (November 1916), 41

HOW BALLAD WRITING AFFECTS
OUR SENIORS

Oh, I've never writ a ballad
And I'd rather eat shrimp salad,
(Tho' the Lord knows how I hate the
   Pink and scrunchy little beasts),
But Miss Dixon says I gotto—
(And I pretty near forgotto)
But I'm sitting at my table
   And my feet are pointing east.

Now one stanza, it is over—
Oh! Heck, what rhymes with "over"?
Ah! yes; "I'm now in clover,"
But when I've got that over
I don't yet know what to write.
I might write of young Lloyd Boyle,
Sturdy son of Irish soil,
But to write of youthful Boyle
Would involve increasing toil,
For there is so much material
I'd never get it done.

Somewhere in this blessed metre
There's a crook. The stanzas peter
Out before I get them started
   Just like that one did, just then.
But I'll keep a-writing on
Just in hope some thought will strike me.
When it does, I'll let it run
   Just in splashes off my pen.

(Wish that blamed idea would come.)
I've been writing for two pages,
But it seems like countless ages,
   For I've scribbled and I've scribbled,

But I haven't said a thing.
This is getting worse each minute,
For whatever I put in it
   I shall have to read before the English class.

'Know where I would like to be—
Just a-lyin' 'neath a tree
Watchin' clouds up in the sky—
Fleecy clouds a-sailin' by
And we'd look up in the blue—
Only me, an' maybe you.
I could write a ballad then
That would drip right off my pen.
     (Aw, shucks!)
For the future I shall promise
  (If you let me live this time),
I'll ne'er write another ballad—
   Never venture into rhyme.

                      —E. H., '17.

———————

XXIII (March 1917), 22

THE WORKER

Ernest Hemingway, '17

Far down in the sweltering guts of the ship
   The stoker swings his scoop
Where the jerking hands of the steam gauge drive
And muscles and tendons and sinews rive;
While it's hotter than hell to a man alive,
   He toils in his sweltering coop.

He is baking and sweating his life away
   In that blasting roar of heat;
But he's fighting a battle with wind and tide,
All to the end that you may ride;
And through it all he is living beside;
   He can work and sleep and eat.

———————

XXIII (March 1917), 39

ATHLETIC VERSE

Ernest Hemingway, '17, and Fred Wilcoxen, '17

THE TACKLE

TWO big red fists pawing the air,
   A drawn, sweat-stained face,
Tufts of blonde hair sticking out of a yellow
        headguard,
   Long gorilla arms, reaching and reaching,
A heaving, gasping chest,
   Alert, shifting mud-stained legs.
A quick pull, a thrust, a headlong dive at a
Group of rushing legs.
   A crashing, rocking jar,
And the crowd yells:
   "Yeah! Threw him for a two yard loss!"

THE PUNT

Twenty-two mud-daubed figures battling together
   on a muddy field.
   A sharp barking of numbers,
The front line of figures pile up together,
The back line crouch and throw themselves
   At the men coming through.
The sodden thump of a pigskin being kicked,
   And the ball rises higher and higher in the air
While the grimy, muddy figures race down the
        field.

THE SAFETY MAN

Standing, a little figure alone in the middle of a
        white-lined field,
Two stands full of faces rise to their feet with
   A mighty roar.

A grey figure whirls free of the tumbled line of
    scrimmage.
  He tears straight down the field,
His flying feet thudding over the white lines.
The safety man poises, then shoots forward;
  He brings the grey sweatered man to the ground
    with a crash.
Cole is on the job.

XXIII (March 1917), 46

THE INEXPRESSIBLE
Ernest Hemingway, '17

When the June bugs were a-circlin'
   Round the arc light on the corner
And a-makin' shooty shadows on the street;
   When you strolled along barefooted
Through a warm dark night of June
     Where the dew from off the cool grass bathed
       your feet—

When you heard a banjo thunkin'
   On the porch across the road,
And you smelled the scent of lilacs in the park
   There was something struggling in you
That you couldn't put in words—
   You was really livin' poetry in the dark!

Senior Tabula 1917, 57–62

CLASS PROPHECY
Ernest Hemingway, '17

"GO over to that table and take the news as it comes from the front," said General Wilcoxen to me. I seated myself at the radio table in the headquarters and adjusted the phones to my ears. Clickety, click, click, click, click, click went the receivers.

"Read it off to me as it comes in," said General Wilcoxen, and I read off the messages as rapidly as possible.

"Dale Bumstead, great powder magnate, captured and held for ransom by the Germans. Shall we pay the $2,000,-000 asked for his return?"

"Don't ask foolish questions," snapped the general.

"General Taylor, Major Swanson and Colonel Rawls have been recommended to command the new expeditionary force. Have you any choice which is the best?"

"Say there is no choice," growled the commander-in-chief."

"There's a man from outside that wants to take some pictures," said a sentry, saluting as he ushered in a familiar looking figure.

"Why, Tom Hildebrand, go as far as you like," said the general, and Tom immediately departed to send a wire to his wife, Ruth Bramberg, who had him report every night what he had done during the day.

The radio clicked again and I wrote down the message for the general. "The following Red Cross nurses have been recommended for the cross of exceptional bravery: Edna Hildman, Ina Peterson, Helen Sinclair and Mabel Tate."

"That's wonderful," said the general. "Give 'em each the double cross."

A loud noise and commotion started outside, and I hastened to the door. "Let me come in and see him. I know him. He'll be glad to see me. Let me in."

110

I reached the door in time to see the sleuth with his bayonet pressed against the rotund stomach of Mr. Le Roy Huxham, the Rip Van Winkle of the class.

"Hux, of all people! What have you been doing with yourself?" gasped Fred.

"Oh, nothing. Just dropped in to see you, old top."

"Sit down, old man, and tell us the news." Knowing Hux, I lay down on a camp cot, prepared for a long session.

"Well," he began, "out of our old bunch of '17, had you heard about Dick and Henry Bredfield fighting a duel over Florence Winder? They both were shot, and Flossie died of a broken heart. You heard about the big war time athletic benefit, didn't you? Pete Chase won the back stroke, Grimm the quarter mile, and Preucil the national tennis title.

"You remember Jack Lander, don't you? Well, old Jasper has started a new religion called Jazzism, and Peaslee and Art Thexton are his favorite disciples. His cult is the biggest sensation since the collapse of the anti-prohibition party that died when Otto Voëlzke, its founder, met his untimely death by drowning.

"Jean Ford, you remember, the Sand Man, has gone into the sugar business and is making a fortune out of which she generously supports Earle Pashley, who lost his mind while writing editorials for Oak Park's greatest weekly news magazine.

"Martha Whitlock's teaching English back at old O. P. H. S. She and Mr. Gehlman, who now has white hair, have many talks about old times. Saw Shorney, too, when I was back visiting. He hands out the checks at the lunch line now, and so many people call him Gordon that it's become as familiar a name as James used to be. He kids the teachers just as the colonel did, too. Say, I saw some show down at the Oak Park when I was back. Neil, Glass, Hahn and Hancock took a night off from the Olympic and gave a benefit performance for the Rev. Bob Sasseman's mission. Say, they were there! They're billed as the 'Kissome Maidens' "——but here Hux grew incoherent and we offered him a lamp, from which he drained the alcohol at one gulp.

"Wait a minute while I get my breath," he gasped. "Here! look at this paper."

The noted octogenarian shoved a copy of the "Examiner" at me and the following item struck me in the eye:

Barton Sisters Sway City—Thousands Answer Call of Gospel—Rum Is on the Run.

Down in the corner was this notice: "The following prominent citizens have decided to move since the passing of the anti-trust law: Mr. Clarence Kohler, head of the potato corporation; Mr. Lyman Worthington, newspaper magnate; Mr. Robert Cole, of the Affiliated Association of Affluence; Mr. Louis Albee, the wealthy scientist."

Turning to the next page, I saw in big type:

"PRES. OHLSEN SAYS WAR MUST CEASE. NOTED HARVARD HEAD DEMANDS CESSATION OF HOSTILITIES.

"WAR WILL GO ON."

"Well," said Fred, "The firm is on the job."

In the second column was this scare head:

"GIRL BANDITS NABBED. WANZER, REID AND NISSEN TAKEN AFTER DESPERATE STRUGGLE.

"Chief of Police Porch Complimented."

"Gee! Paul always could get the girls," said Hux, who was rapidly regaining strength.

"Powers Wallops Cards With Four-Ply Swat. Kenney, Rehm, and Thor score on Homer.

"Wagenknecht Pitches Good Game," were the big heads on the first sport page.

"Good for Lib," yelled General W., looking over my shoulder, and casting my eye on the next page, I read:

"Kimball knocks out Von Pein in championship bout."

"Feminine featherweight title changes hands."

"Hurray," yelled Hux. "I win ten bucks. Let's go out and take in a show."

As our concentration camp was located on the lake front, we were compelled to walk past the place where Hale Printup saved his city by firing hot air at the Zeppelins. We removed our hats as we passed the spot, as all of us recalled vividly the tragic scene of Printup's fiery end when his jaws united from the friction.

"What shall we see?" said Hux. "Les Shaw and his tame lions are at the Hippodrome. Betty Brydon's known as 'Charlotte the Second'; Ruth Morrison's got Sousa's old job, and Zelma Owen trains the chorus. Then over at the Illinois Roberta Finnell is playing leads with Herbert Tree's grandson. Or, don't you feel equal to a little Shakespeare? Ada Meservey sings the title role in 'Madame Butterfly' tonight at the Auditorium. K. Bagley used to be called the second Pavlowa, but now the only reason Pavlowa's remembered is because she's been compared with K."

"Oh, let's go in and see Edith Treleaven and Ed Willcox in 'The Green Peril,'" suggested the economical Wilcoxen.

Loretta Below shoved us three pasteboards from behind the wicket. We entered to see the flickering trials of Ed and Edith for four reels. This was followed by a Musselman Mutual, produced by Wirth, photographed by Eichelberg. Cheer after cheer rocked the house during this picture, and the police had to be called in to carry out the members of the audience who had swooned with laughter.

The next film featured Dorothy Estabrook in the "Crimes of Catherine," with Wayne Brandstadt playing the villain.

A Pathe news came next, featuring the wedding of Sue Lowrey and Frank Lee, the preparedness kindergarten conducted by Chester Iverson, Margaret Wright and Flora Konald, and the first woman submarine diver, Dorothy Willard.

As we left the theater a boy came up selling Saturday Evening Posts.

"Hello, Myron," said Fred, and I recognized the W. K. Capouch, who was reported to have made a million in that questionable enterprise. We gave Capouch a quarter and received 15 cents in change.

On the cover of the Saturday Evening Post was a very familiar face, but I did not seem quite able to place it.

"Why," said Hux, "that's Dorothy Hollands. Kendall

draws her face on all his magazine covers. Poor Golder! he nearly goes mad with rage whenever he sees a Post being walked on or destroyed."

Clang! clang! went a patrol wagon up the street, and we followed on a run. A swarm of bluecoats crowded out and into a large stone front house and immediately reappeared hustling a crowd of fashionably dressed ladies into the wagon. "Look! they've got Helen Cirese, Edith Buehler, Kathryn Clinton and Marion Campbell! That's the Ladies' Fraternal Bridge Club that Inspector Clifford has been threatening to raid for so long." A burly red-faced figure climbed onto the driver's seat and pushed in the clutch. "Oh, Wales," I called. "Very good, Sherry," he answered, and the wagon went on its way with Helen Veach, the motorcycle copette, sputtering along in its wake.

"Say! I've seen those white wings before somewhere," said Hux, pointing at five street cleaners who were busily pushing the dust up into their scoops. He whistled and one of them raised his head. It was Charles Campbell. He waved merrily and nudged his companions, and we were surprised to see the countenances of Joel Crissey, Frank Duennes, Dick Craig, and Hilly Gage.

"Speed up there. Here's the 'cop,'" growled a voice, and turning, we were surprised to see Bud Bethell. "Yes, women fill a lot of men's places now," she said. "Go into that office building across the street and you'll see a bunch of the old crowd."

We thanked Bud and barely got across the street in front of a speeding Ford driven by M. Hemingway, the noted lady veterinarian. As the car whizzed by us it struck an elderly lady who was crossing the street and hurled her senseless to the pavement. Hastening to her aid, we found it to be Jessie Brown! "Who done it?" she gasped. "Doc Hemingway," Fred replied. "I knew she'd get me finally," wheezed Jessie, and passed away. We carried her lifeless body into the office building and nearly tripped over Carroll Dyrenforth, who was industriously scrubbing the steps. "Oh, take her right in," said Carroll, "I'll call a bellboy," and at her ring Gertrude Early, Edith Ebersold and Grace Dabbert appeared attired in their snappy livery and gently took the body upstairs.

114

After that gruesome occurrence I felt a trifle shaky, and so we stopped in at Wright's, where Laura, who is a member of the firm, personally served us some good old Dolan Doughnuts, the kind that made such a reputation for Jeff's string of restaurants.

As we munched the doughnuts and drank our coffee we glanced through a copy of "Vanity Fair" that Florence Caldwell was making such a success with since Gerald Andrews wrote his famous novel, "What's in the Cup," as a serial for her publication. Frank Julius had a good theatrical review in the magazine, but Charles Jacobs' fashion plates were what all the ladies were gazing at.

"Say," said Laura, "listen a minute," as she came out from the kitchen and stood at our table to chat over old times. "Did you hear about Ruth Swanson's persuading old Bill Haupt to leave his million-dollar shoe business to her, and about Jean Avery eloping with Roland Rodeck?"

"No," I marveled, but Laura went on: "That's nothing! Had you heard about Cora Andrew and Herm Kellberg? My! that was a sensation, and in a public aeroplane, too! It's been the talk of the city. Why, it's the biggest thing since Olga Flohr won the Kentucky Derby.

"And did you hear about Ig Smeeth and Glenn Privat and Allen Speelman starting a matrimonial bureau? They've got the biggest business in the city and they've made some simply stupendous matches. The famous Walter Blount and Alice Carlson and Frances Bumsted and poor old tottering Frank Reid, the dumb wonder. Oh, there have been millions implicated in those matches.

"Say, did you know Irving Ellis is still in school? He gets his Latin out of one of the new ponies that Noel Parris has put out, too. He told me all about it. He says maybe he'll graduate next year, but the students are petitioning him to stay, because they won't recognize the high school without him."

"Howdy, Laura. Megga Murk and bossy in the bowl, draw one. Well, Max, how are you?" It was Shep, the great Northwestern football coach.

"Sure," he said. "I come in here often. It's just across the street from where Helen and I have our flat. She keeps house for me since the divorce. I was sorry to see

old Kohler go to the bad. Well, I gotta beat it. Seen tonight's American?" He shoved us the pink sheet and strode
out through the swinging doors.

"LOVERS DIE IN SUICIDE PACT.
PROMINENT ATTORNEY AND SOCIETY MAIDEN
SHOT; LULL AND JOHNSON FAMILIES
PROSTRATED."

"Poor Deak," said Fred, "But they're happy now."

In another column were the words,

"FEMININE BUTCHERS SHOW HEROISM."
HOLD STEERS AT BAY WHILE CROWD ESCAPES.
MOCKLER, SCHWAB AND SULTENMEYER OPPOSE
INFURIATED ANIMALS.

"At noon yesterday in the stockyards, while the Ger-
mo-Austrian Peace commission was being entertained,
infuriated steers broke loose from herders and charged
the distinguished crowd of spectators. Misses Marguerite
Mockler, Janet Schwab and Elsie Sultenmeyer grasped
the pitchforks which were lying on the ground, and hero-
ically drove the animals back to the pens. Philip White, a
prominent coal dealer, who was present, then showed his
presence of mind by shutting the gate and imprisoning
the animals.

"Those in the committee of entertainment who were
perilled were:

"Mr. and Mrs. Edward Wilson, head of the committee
of welcome,

"Mr. Charles Kilmer, American Ambassador to the
Danish West Indies,

"Miss Gladys Johnson, the head of Hull House.

"Misses Marion Campbell and Helen Smith, noted
policewomen,

"Mrs. Darthea Haines Murray, wife of Gen. William
Murray, commander of the French Division, and

"Mr. Irving Lobstein and Mr. Maurice Loven of Loven
and Lobstein, who negotiated the Franco-American loan."

Our hearts were so full of pride at the thought that we
had known those heroines, that we left the lunch room
without even thinking of paying our check.

Passing up the street, past the Wyne Yardley Zimmer-

116

man coal company's warehouse, we nearly bumped into Connie Lockyer, who was hurrying along carrying a small satchel. "Get out of my way, quick," she hissed. "Jack's running at the 2nd Regiment, and I've got to get there in time to get him started. I'm managing him now."

A boy stopped us at the corner. "Get your copy of Pomeroy's Popular History of the U.S.! Nearly all sold out; only a few left. Get 'em here." "All about Willie Ehrman's winning the doubles at Newport. Last edition." Seeing my bald head, a man whom I at once recognized as Johnny Nelson approached. Buy a bottle of Isabel Krantz's hair restorer and beautifier! All the famous beauties recommend it. Marion Kraft and Marie Kelly endorse it. Just give it a trial! It'll grow hair on a turnip or a boiled onion."

We hailed a taxi to escape the hair restorer and told Marion Thoms, the driver, to take us to the Smith-Stone, now our leading hotel.

Seated at a table were Inez Parsal, Mildred Mills and Florence Miller, nearly bursting their gloves encoring Louise Lucas' dancing.

Margaret Ruddiman brought us in a couple of (censored) and a package of (censored) and we were soon contentedly enjoying life.

"Stien," said General Fred, "We've seen 'em all."

"Every one," said Hux.

"All except two," I said.

"They probably saw us first," said the general.

"No, it's Pentecost and King."

"Let's look 'em up in the Directory," said Hux. I called a waiter and soon we were poring over its pages.

"Here it is!" cried Fred.

"J. Pentecost and H. King, Chicken Farmers,"

"We might have known it," Hux said.

Well, here's luck to you and to the grand old class. Long may it wave! Do you think they'll kick us out if we gave the class yell? Let's risk it all right, Seniors!

APPENDIX

Material About Ernest Hemingway in *The Trapeze* and *The Tabula*.
Compiled by Daniel Reichard, Oak Park and River Forest High School

The Trapeze

"What Would One Look Like, If He Had," 29 February 1916, 2. Hemingway's dimples.

"Orchestra Scores Success in Martha," 4 May 1916, 1. Hemingway played the cello.

"The Trapeze Staff," 25 May 1916, 1. Staff photo included Hemingway.

"Oak Park Smothers Proviso," 27 October 1916, 3. Hemingway played right guard.

"Air Line," 27 October 1916, 4. Joke about Hemingway.

"Championship Form in New Trier Game," 3 November 1916, 1. Hemingway played left guard.

"Personals," 3 November 1916, 3. Hemingway member of Trap Shooting Club.

"Personals," 10 November 1916, 3. Hemingway attended party.

"Freak Election Bets In Evidence Monday," 17 November 1916, 1. Hemingway lost bet.

"Wanted—A New Yell By the Senior Class," 17 November 1916, 1. Hemingway on Yell Committee.

"Oak Park Victors," 17 November 1916, 3. Hemingway played right guard.

"Notes on Toledo Trip," 17 November 1916, 3. Hemingway went with football team.

"Personals," 17 November 1916, 3. Hemingway in Trap Shooting Club; Hemingway lost election bet.

"Air Line," 17 November 1916, 4. Joke about Hemingway.

"Personals," 24 November 1916 3. Hemingway competed in Trap Shooting Club.

"Great Meeting Reported at Older Boys Confab," 8 December 1916, 2. Hemingway attended Galesburg conference.

"Burke Club Resurrected For Season of Rangling," 8 December 1916, 3. Hemingway temporary secretary.

"Monograms Are Awarded Athletes," 15 December 1916, 1. Hemingway won minor monogram.

"Athletic Notes," 15 December 1916, 2. Hemingway candidate for track manager.

"Large Crowd Out for Basketball Teams," 15 December 1916, 2. Hemingway played intra-school basketball.

"Personals," 22 December 1916, 3. Hemingway in Trap Shooting Club.

"Phelps, Boyle and Hemingway Elected," 19 January 1917, 1. Hemingway elected track manager.

"Senior to Give Party for Freshmen Tonight," 19 January 1917, 1. Hemingway on program.

"Burke Club Starts New Year With Hot Debate," 19 January 1917, 2. Hemingway debated.

"The Class Play Drawing Near," 2 February 1917, 1. Hemingway to play Sheridan in *Beau Brummel*.

"Gun Club Defeats Evanstons and Wilmette in Triangle Meet," 2 February 1917, 1. Hemingway competed.

"Oak Park Natators Are Defeated by Evanston Swimmers," 2 February 1917, 3. Hemingway plunged.

"Natators to Meet New Trier Tonight," 9 February 1917, 1. Hemingway to plunge.

"Curtain to Rise on Play Tonight," 16 February 1917, 1. Hemingway in play.

"Oak Park Natators Lose to New Trier," 16 February 1917, 1. Hemingway plunged.

"Oak Park Defeats LaGrange in Track," 23 February 1917, 1. Hemingway managed team.

"Beau Brummel Complete Success," 23 February 1917, 1. Hemingway acted.

"Swimming Team Is Defeated By Evanston," 23 February 1917, 2. Hemingway plunged.

"Who's Who in Beau Brummel?" 23 February 1917, 3. Hemingway on Hemingway.

"Personal," 23 February 1917, 3. Hemingway on Commercial Law honor roll.

"Commercial AA Students," 2 March 1917, 2. Hemingway on Commercial Law honor roll.

"Personals," 2 March 1917, 3. Hemingway hosted tea.

"New Trier Tankers Win From Locals," 2 March 1917, 4. Hemingway on water basketball team.

"St Patrick Tabula Is Coming Soon," 9 March 1917, 1. Hemingway to contribute.

"Senate to Hold Session in Assembly," 16 March 1917, 1. Hemingway to debate.

"Oak Park Shows Well in Big Swim," 23 March 1917, 1. Hemingway plunged; elected captain of water basketball team.

"Senate Meets Before Students in Assembly," 23 March 1917, 2. Hemingway debated.

"Athletic Notes," 23 March 1917, 4. Hemingway elected captain.

"Regulars Trounce Mud Hens," 23 March 1917, 4. Hemingway played spring football.

"Water Basketball New Sport," 30 March 1917, 1. Hemingway on team.

"Athletic Notes," 30 March 1917, 4. Hemingway captain of water basketball; went to Culver as track manager.

120

"Oak Park Splashers Against Crane Tonight,"
20 April 1917, 3. Hemingway to plunge and
on water basketball team.

"Oak Park Tankers Duck Crane 51-8," 27 April
1917, 1. Hemingway plunged and on water
basketball team.

"Air Line," 27 April 1917, 4. Joke about Hemingway.

"Faculty Chooses Commencement Speakers,"
27 April 1917, 4. Hemingway to give class
prophecy.

"Swimming Team Closes Season," 4 May 1917,
3. Hemingway on team.

"Personal," 4 May 1917, 3. Hemingway competed
with Shot Gun Club.

"Tabula-Trapeze Subscription Campaign
Started," 11 May 1917, 1. Hemingway
participated.

"Shot Gun Club News," 11 May 1917, 3. Hemingway competed.

"Air Line," 11 May 1917, 4. Joke about Hemingway.

"Trapeze Staff," 25 May 1917, 1. Staff photo
included Hemingway.

"Senior College Plans Presented," 25 May 1917,
1. Hemingway to attend University of
Illinois.

"Class Day Coming," 25 May 1917, 2. Hemingway to write class prophecy.

"Personal," 14 December 1917, 2. Hemingway
on *Star*.

"O. P. At the Front," 12 April 1918, 4. Hemingway on strike duty with National Guard.

"O. P. at the Front," 17 May 1918, 4. Hemingway in Ambulance Corps and war corre-
spondent.

"O.P. at the Front," 24 May 1918, 4. Hemingway promoted.

"O.P. at the Front," 13 December 1918, 4.
Hemingway left hospital to help Italian
drive.

121

"Hanna Club Has Rousing First Meeting With 'Ernie' Hemingway as Speaker," 7 February 1919, 2. Hemingway spoke on war.

"Hemingway Speaks to High School" 21 March 1919, 1. Hemingway spoke on war at Assembly.

The Tabula

"Major Football," XXIII (November 1916), 30. Right tackle.

"Swimming," XXIII (March 1917), 38. Plunger.

"*Senior Tabula 1917*, cartoons about Hemingway's swimming and diving, 138 & 147.

Photoes of Hemingway in the Senior Tabula

1914, p. 105—Rifle Club

1915, p. 99—*Trapeze* Staff

  p. 101—Burke Club

  p. 121—Minor Football

1917, p. 23—Senior photo, with activities

  p. 49—Class Day speaker

  p. 83—Cast of *Beau Brummel*

  p. 91—*Trapeze* Staff

  p. 93—Burke Club

  p. 107—Boy's High School Club

  p. 119—Major Football

  p. 131—Track

  p. 133—Swimming

  p. 134—Hanna Club